Cooking with Quorn: 50 Meals from Around The World

MARK GREEN

Copyright © 2014 Mark Green

All rights reserved.

ISBN-10: 1500715387
ISBN-13: 978-1500715380

DEDICATION

For my Mum, who gave me my first cookbook - "More Easy Cooking For One or Two" by Louise Davies - just before she packed me off to university.

CONTENTS

Introduction 8

Nutrition and Diet 9

Cooking Tips and Metric Conversions 13

American (Hot) Pepperoni Pizza 14

Southern Fried Quorn Fillets 17

Carbonnade à la Flamande avec Frites 19

Quorn and Cashew Nuts with Rice 22

Quorn Chow Mein 24

Quorn Fried Rice 26

Sweet and Sour Quorn 28

Bangers and Mash in Red Wine Gravy 30

Cornish Pasty 32

Cottage Pie 34

Full English Breakfast 36

Lancashire Hotpot 38

Quorn in Ale Pudding 40

Toad in the Hole 43

Traditional Sunday Roast with Yorkshire Pudding 45

Quorn Bourguignonne with Dauphinois Potatoes 48

Quorn au Pot with Boulangère Potatoes 51

Quorn au Vin with Lyonnaise Potatoes 54

Tartiflette 57

Moussaka 59

Hungarian Goulash 62

Paprika Quorn Fillets	64
Quorn Biryani	66
Quorn Korma with Pilau Rice and Naan Bread	68
Quorn Madras with Bombay Potatoes	71
Quorn Tikka Masala with Rice and Naan Bread	73
Quorn Vindaloo	76
Tandoori Quorn with Saffron Rice	78
Irish Stew and Dumplings	80
Italian Casserole with Risotto alla Milanese	82
Lasagna al Forno	84
Quorn Risotto	87
Spaghetti Bolognese	89
Tagliatelle Carbonara	91
Chilli con Quorn with Guacamole	93
Mole Quorn	96
Quorn Fajitas	98
Moroccan Spicy Tagine with Flatbread	101
Bitterballen	104
Quorn Stroganoff	106
Haggis wi' 'tatties an' 'neeps	108
Singapore Stir Fried Noodles	111
Basque Quorn	113
Paella	115
Rösti mit Spiegel Ei	117
Green Curry with Sticky Rice	119
Pad Thai	121

Red Curry with Jasmine Rice 123

Stuffed Peppers 125

Vietnamese Noodle Soup 127

Index 129

Appendix: Comparing Quorn with Beef, Chicken and Pork 148

Introduction

During my years of globe-trotting, which has taken me to more than 60 countries, one of my greatest pleasures has been to try the local dishes wherever I go. As someone who turned veggie after 30 years of enjoying meat, I am one of those who now uses Quorn as a substitute.

In this book I have gathered together some of my favourite dishes from around the world and reproduced them here with Quorn in place of the original meat. This necessitates some changes to the recipes to cope with the peculiarities of cooking with Quorn, notably its tendency to dry out if overcooked.

My aim is to take you on a culinary journey around the world. I hope you enjoy the meals along the way.

If you have any feedback, comments, or favourite recipes of your own, I would be delighted to hear from you. You can reach me at:

markr_green@msn.com

Nutrition and Diet

Quorn is a good source of protein that is low in fats, in particular saturated fats. This makes it a great part of a healthy diet. For a direct comparison of the nutritional content of Quorn with beef, chicken and pork I have included this as an appendix.

Vegetarian Diet

It goes without saying that Quorn is suitable for a vegetarian diet. All of the meals included in this book are suitable for vegetarians – except the Paella which contains seafood along with the Quorn fillets and Quorn Chorizo sausage (but it is such a great tasting recipe and is okay for pescetarians so I've included it anyway).

I have used beef and chicken stock cubes in some of the recipes but if you prefer to use vegetable stock cubes instead then that will work well too.

Gluten Free Diet

The recipes are also suitable for gluten free diets except those listed below:

- American (Hot) Pepperoni Pizza
- Bitterballen
- Cornish Pasty
- Irish Stew with Dumplings (unless you leave out the dumplings and the pearl barley)
- Quorn in Ale Pudding
- Quorn Fajitas (unless you make the tortillas with corn flour)
- Southern Fried Quorn Fillets
- Toad in the Hole
- Traditional Sunday Roast with Yorkshire Pudding (unless you leave out the Yorkshire Pudding and stuffing and use corn flour to thicken the gravy)

The following recipes can be adapted for a gluten free diet by using corn flour to thicken the sauces or gravy:

- Haggis wi' 'tatties an' 'neeps
- Moussaka
- Paprika Quorn Fillets
- Quorn au Pot with Boulangère Potatoes
- Quorn au Vin with Lyonnaise Potatoes
- Quorn Korma with Pilau Rice and Naan Bread

The following recipes can be adapted for a gluten free diet by leaving out the breads:

- Carbonnade à la Flamande avec Frites
- Full English Breakfast
- Moroccan Spicy Tagine with Flatbread
- Quorn Korma with Pilau Rice and Naan Bread
- Quorn Tikka Masala with Rice and Naan Bread

The following recipes may be made with gluten free pasta:

- Lasagna al Forno (and use corn flour in sauce)
- Spaghetti Bolognese
- Tagliatelle Carbonara

The following recipes may be made with rice noodles in place of the egg noodles:

- Quorn Chow Mein
- Vietnamese Noodle Soup

The following recipes contain soy sauce which is made from wheat. There is some debate whether the process of fermenting the beans to make the soy sauce breaks down the gluten making it safe for those who need to follow a gluten free diet:

- Quorn with Cashew Nuts and Rice
- Quorn Chow Mein
- Quorn Fried Rice
- Singapore Stir Fried Noodles
- Sweet and Sour Quorn

Dairy Free Diet

You can eat Quorn if you are lactose intolerant but the following recipes include milk, yoghurt or cream so you will need to avoid them, unless you substitute soya milk or similar for the milk called for in the recipe:

- Bangers and Mash with Red Wine Gravy (but you can omit the cream from the mashed potatoes)
- Bitterballen
- Chilli con Quorn with Guacamole (but you can just serve without the soured cream on top and it is still delicious)
- Cottage Pie (but you can omit the cream and cheese from the mashed

potato topping)
- Haggis wi' 'tatties an' 'neeps (but you can omit the cream from the mashed potatoes)
- Hungarian Goulash
- Lasagna al Forno
- Moussaka
- Paprika Quorn Fillets
- Quorn Biryani
- Quorn Bourguignonne with Dauphinois Potatoes (but you can substitute other types of potatoes from different recipes that don't include milk or cream)
- Quorn Fajitas (but you can just serve it without the soured cream)
- Quorn Korma with Pilau Rice and Naan Bread
- Quorn au Pot with Boulangère Potatoes (but again you can substitute other types of potatoes from recipes that don't include milk or cream)
- Quorn Stroganoff
- Quorn Tikka Masala with Rice and Naan Bread
- Quorn Vindaloo (but you can leave out the yoghurt dressing)
- Tandoori Quorn with Saffron Rice
- Tartiflette
- Toad in the Hole
- Traditional Sunday Roast with Yorkshire Pudding (but you can leave out the Yorkshire Pudding)

Nut/Peanut allergies

Only two of the recipes use peanuts and both have suitable workarounds to avoid the risk of an allergic reaction:

- Mole Quorn (but you can make it without the peanut butter and it will still have the exotic Mexican taste)
- Pad Thai (substitute sesame seeds for the crushed roast peanut garnish)

Reduced Salt Diet

I tend to cook without using salt. None of the recipes here include salt (except in the various breads and the Vindaloo marinade) and they taste great this way. But, if you like to season your cooking with salt as well as pepper, then feel free to do so according to your own taste.

The following dishes use soy sauce, Thai fish sauce or Oyster sauce, all of which contain high levels of salt – although reduced salt varieties are available:

- Green Curry with Sticky Rice
- Pad Thai
- Quorn and Cashew Nuts with Rice
- Quorn Chow Mein
- Quorn Fried Rice
- Red Curry with Jasmine Rice
- Singapore Stir Fried Noodles
- Sweet and Sour Quorn

Butter or Margerine

In keeping with the vegetarian approach, I have used margerine throughout this book but you could just as easily use butter if you prefer.

Sunflower oil, olive oil, groundnut oil

I have used sunflower oil throughout this book as my cooking oil.

Some dishes, notably those from Mediterranean countries such as Italy, Greece, Spain and Turkey could be made with olive oil – indeed many would argue this gives them a more authentic taste. Personally I prefer to use olive oil in dressings but not for cooking as I find it tends to smoke at lower temperatures than sunflower oil.

For oriental dishes, many will prefer to use groundnut oil as a more traditional cooking oil. This will work very well with the recipes in this book – though of course you need to be aware of potential risks for nut allergy sufferers.

Cooking Tips and Metric Conversions

The cooking times are all based on using ingredients at room temperature or chilled rather than frozen. Quorn is often sold in frozen packs and is great to keep in your freezer so I expect many of you will be cooking with Quorn from your freezer. I have found that Quorn defrosts very quickly and so the cooking time for most of the meals are hardly affected if you use Quorn taken straight from the freezer – maybe add a minute or two when cooking Quorn mince, for example.

I tend to remove Quorn fillets from the freezer about half an hour before I want to cook with them. The same goes for frozen Quorn sausages though when I am in a hurry I do microwave them for 30 seconds on the defrost setting to help the thawing process.

Cooking is more of an art than a science anyway so you will need to see what works for you in your kitchen with your pans and your hob and oven.

I have used metric measures throughout (grammes and millilitres) but for those who are used to Imperial measures, here is a quick (approximate) conversion chart:

100g = 3.5 oz
500g = 17.5 oz

1 oz = 30g
1 lb = 450g

100ml = 3.5 fl oz
500ml = 0.9 pints or 17.5 fl oz (or 1.05 US pints)
1 l = 1.8 pints or 35 fl oz (2.1 US pints)

1 fl oz = 30ml
1 pint = 570ml
1 US pint = 475ml

American (Hot) Pepperoni Pizza

The classic American take on this Italian speciality. Have it Hot, with chilli in the sauce, or Not, omitting the chilli – whichever you prefer.

INGREDIENTS (makes a 9 inch diameter pizza)

For the base:
Strong white flour (150g)
Dried Yeast (1 tspn)
Sugar (½ tspn)
Salt (1 tspn)
Water (100ml)

For the sauce:
Plum Tomatoes (400g tin, chopped)
Tomato purée double concentrate (1 tbspn)
Onion (1 small)
Oregano (1 tspn)
Garlic (1 clove)
Sunflower oil (1 tbspn)
Bird's eye chilli (1 optional)

Black pepper

For the topping:
Quorn Pepperoni (8-10 slices)
Green Pepper
Mozzarella cheese (50g grated)
Olive oil (1 tbspn)

You will need a mixing bowl, a large saucepan and a baking tray.

Time required: 2 hours 15 minutes (including 15 minutes for yeast to begin to activate, 1 hour for dough to rise and 15 minutes standing time for prepared pizza before baking!)

1. Dissolve sugar in hand-hot water. Add dried yeast and stir. Leave for 10-15 minutes until approximately ½ cm of froth has built up on top of liquid.

2. Mix flour and salt in bowl. Gradually add liquid to mix, stirring with fork. Mix dough until all flour is incorporated into dough leaving sides of bowl clean.

3. Turn the dough out onto a work-surface and knead for 6-8 minutes, flouring the surface as necessary to prevent it sticking. Dough will become very smooth and elastic. Return kneaded dough to bowl and set aside to rise. This will take about an hour until it more or less doubles in size. You may place the dough in a warmed oven to speed this up.

4. In large saucepan, soften the onion in the sunflower oil over a low heat. Add chopped tomatoes, crushed garlic, oregano and black pepper to taste. Optionally, add bird's eye chilli if you want to have a Hot sauce. Simmer without lid over a low heat, stirring occasionally, until the liquid reduces and you are have a moist, but quite stiff, tomato sauce. This will take between 20 and 30 minutes. Stir in tomato purée about half way through this cooking time.

5. When dough has doubled in size, remove from bowl and roll out to a circle approximately 9 inches in diameter (the size of a dinner plate). Place on baking tray and brush with a little olive oil.

6. Spread tomato sauce over pizza base, leaving a narrow edge uncovered. Cut green pepper horizontally to form rings. Arrange

pepper rings on pizza. Scatter grated mozzarella over pizza. Add Quorn pepperoni slices. Drizzle with olive oil, particularly over the pepperoni slices. Leave to stand for 15 minutes.

7. Turn oven up to 220 degrees Celsius. When it reaches temperature, place baking tray with pizza on shelf in upper half of oven. Bake until edge of pizza turns golden brown (approximately 15 minutes).

8. Serve immediately from the oven.

Calories: 575 kcal per half pizza

Southern Fried Quorn Fillets

The precise blend of herbs and spices in this dish from the southern states of America is often a family secret passed down from mother to daughter. Here is my take on it, but keep it to yourself!

INGREDIENTS (serves 4)

Quorn Fillets (8)
Breadcrumbs (150g)
Cayenne Pepper (2 tspn)
Thyme (1½ tspn)
Oregano (1½ tspn)
Black Pepper
Egg (2 medium)
Potatoes (600g)
Sunflower oil (3 cm deep in deep-frying pan)

You will need a deep-frying pan and a mixing bowl.

Time required: 15 minutes

1. Take Quorn fillets from freezer/refridgerator and allow to thaw – approximately 30 minutes – as frying must be done with defrosted fillets.

2. Heat approximately 3cm of oil in the deep frying pan. It is ready for cooking when a breadcrumb dropped in the oil sizzles. Be careful not to let the oil get too hot – never leave it unattended.

3. Grate bread over a mixing bowl to make breadcrumbs. Add cayenne pepper, thyme and oregano. Season with plenty of black pepper. Mix thoroughly to ensure the herbs and spices are evenly distributed. Turn out onto plate.

4. Cut potatoes into wedges. Carefully lower into hot oil. Cook for approximately 4 minutes until golden brown. Remove from oil and set aside on kitchen roll to absorb excess oil.

5. Beat eggs in clean bowl. Dip Quorn fillets in beaten egg and ensure coated all over.

6. Press Quorn fillets into breadcrumb mix, turning over to ensure they have a crumb-coating all over. Carefully lower Quorn fillets into hot oil. Cook for approximately 4 minutes.

7. Remove cooked Quorn fillets and place on kitchen roll to absorb excess oil.

8. Serve Quorn fillets and potato wedges immediately (taking care to avoid burns from any hot oil.

Calories: 480 kcal per portion

Carbonnade à la Flamande avec Frites

This old Flemish recipe is best made with proper Belgian Beer. I use Leffe Brun for the distinctive flavour it gives the gravy.

INGREDIENTS (serves 4)

Quorn Steak Strips (400g)
Onion (2 large)
Belgian Beer (500ml)
Garlic (1 clove)
Beef stock cube
Thyme (½ tspn dried)
Bay leaf
Mustard powder (1 tspn)
Black pepper
Sunflower oil (1 tbspn)

For the croutons:
French Bread (1 stick)
Olive oil (1 tbspn)
Garlic (1 clove)
Gruyère Cheese (200g)

For the frites:
Potatoes (800g)

You will need a large casserole with a lid, a frying pan and a baking tray.

Time required: 1 hours 25 minutes

1. Pre-heat the oven to 140 degrees Celsius.

2. Heat the sunflower oil in the casserole over a medium high heat. Roughly chop the onions and brown in the oil for 2 minutes. Add the Quorn Steak Strips and finely chopped garlic and continue to fry for further 3 minutes, stirring occasionally.

3. Pour in the beef gradually. Add crumbled beef stock cube, mustard powder, thyme and bay leaf. Season with black pepper. Stir thoroughly. Bring to simmering point. Cover with lid then place in middle shelf of pre-heated oven. Leave to cook undisturbed for 1 hour.

4. Meanwhile cut the French bread into slices about 2.5cm thick. Allow 2 slices per person. Place on baking tray and drizzle with olive oil. Turn the slices over and drizzle other side. Sprinkle finely chopped garlic over slices. Add to middle of oven and cook for 20 minutes. Remove from oven and set aside.

5. When the casserole has been cooking for an hour, remove the lid and allow to cook for further 15 minutes.

6. Peel and cut the potatoes into thin chips. If you have a deep frier then you can cook them in this. You may need to cook them in batches to fit your frier. It should take about 5 minutes per batch. Alternatively you can cook them in a frying pan. I like to shallow fry them in sunflower oil. Heat the pan so that the oil is very hot but not smoking and shallow fry the potatoes in batches so that you have room to flip them and move them around in the pan. Keep turning them constantly so that they fry evenly.

7. Remove chips from oil as soon as they are done and place on kitchen paper to absorb any excess oil. Keep warm in bottom of oven until required.

8. Grate the cheese and pile on top of the baked croutons. When

casserole has finished cooking, remove from oven, place the croutons carefully over the top of the casserole and place under a hot grill to melt the cheese.

9. When the cheese is bubbling, remove from casserole from grill.

10. Carefully spoon out the stew onto plates, keeping the croutons perched on top. Serve immediately with the chips.

Calories: 741 kcal per portion

Quorn and Cashew Nuts with Rice

I love the crunchy texture the cashew nuts give to this traditional Chinese dish. I have made it with Quorn Chicken Pieces but you can easily substitute Quorn Steak Strips and use a beef stock cube to make a tasty alternative.

INGREDIENTS (serves 4)

Quorn Chicken Pieces (300g)
Cashew nuts (100g)
Onion (1 large)
Green Pepper (1 medium)
Bamboo shoots (1 x 120g tin)
Carrot (300g)
Chicken stock cube
Flour (1 tsp, plain)
Soy sauce (1 tbspn, dark)
Sunflower oil (1 tbspn)
Long grain rice (300g)

You will need a wok or large frying pan, a large saucepan and a seive.

Time required: 15 minutes

1. Bring large pan of water to boil. Add rice and return to boil then cover with lid (offset to prevent boiling over). Cook for 10 minutes.

2. Meanwhile, heat the sunflower oil in the wok over a high heat. Fry the Quorn Chicken Pieces Strips for 2 minutes, stirring regularly.

3. Chop the onion into eight pieces. De-seed and chop the green pepper into chunks. Grate the carrot.

4. Add the onion pieces, chopped green pepper, grated carrot and bamboo shoots to the wok. Continue cooking for 2 minutes, stirring regularly.

5. Dissolve the stock cube in 250ml of hot water. Pour steadily into wok. Bring to simmering point. Cook for 2 minutes, stirring regularly.

6. Make up a smooth runny paste of flour and cold water. Pour slowly into wok, stirring continuously. Keep stirring until the flour paste is incorporated into the stock to form a thick gravy.

7. Add soy sauce to the wok and continue cooking for 2 minutes, stirring regularly.

8. Add cashew nuts to the wok and stir in.

9. Drain cooked rice in sieve and spoon into bowls. Spoon the Quorn and cashew nut mix over the rice and serve immediately.

Calories: 705 kcal per portion

Quorn Chow Mein

This classic Chinese dish can be made with either Quorn Steak Strips, as I have done here, or with Quorn Chicken Pieces.

INGREDIENTS (serves 4)

Quorn Steak Strips (400g)
Egg Noodles (325g / 4 nests)
Bean sprouts (200g)
Carrot (300g)
Soy sauce (1 tbspn, dark)
Sunflower oil (1 tbspn)
Spring onion (4)

You will need a wok or large frying pan and a large saucepan.

Time required: 15 minutes

1. Bring large pan of water to boil. Add noodles and return to boil then cover with lid (offset to prevent boiling over). Cook for 4 minutes.

2. Heat the sunflower oil in the wok over a medium high heat. Fry the Quorn Steak Strips for 2 minutes, stirring regularly.

3. Add the bean sprouts and fry for 2 minutes, stirring regularly.

4. Drain the noodles. Add to the wok and cook for 2 minutes, stirring regularly.

5. Grate the carrot and add to the wok. Continue cooking for 2 minutes, stirring regularly.

6. Add soy sauce to the wok and continue cooking for 3 minutes, stirring regularly.

7. Serve the chow mein in bowls. Garnish with chopped spring onion.

Calories: 519 kcal per portion

Quorn Fried Rice

This simple Chinese dish can be made any time. You can use Quorn Steak Strips, as I have done here, or alternatively, try it with Quorn Chicken Pieces.

INGREDIENTS (serves 4)

Quorn Steak Strips (400g)
Egg (2)
Long grain Rice (300g)
Peas (100g)
Soy sauce (1 tbspn, dark)
Sunflower oil (1 tbspn)
Spring onion (4)

You will need a wok or large frying pan, a large saucepan and a sieve.

Time required: 20 minutes

1. Bring large pan of water to boil. Add rice and return to boil then cover with lid (offset to prevent boiling over). Cook for 10 minutes.

2. Heat the sunflower oil in the wok over a medium high heat. Fry the Quorn Steak Strips for 2 minutes, stirring regularly. Remove from the wok and set aside.

3. Drain the cooked rice.

4. Beat the eggs then pour into wok, stirring constantly. Within seconds the eggs will start to form into a scrambled egg mix. Immediately add the peas and return the beef to the wok. Stir together and cook for 1 minute.

5. Add the cooked rice to the wok and cook for 3 minutes, stirring constantly to mix the ingredients thoroughly.

6. Add soy sauce to the wok and continue cooking for 3 minutes, stirring regularly.

7. Serve in bowls. Garnish with chopped spring onion.

Calories: 551 kcal per portion

Sweet and Sour Quorn

I love the contrasting flavours in this Chinese recipe. Some people like to prepare their "meat" in batter but I've gone for the healthy option and simply stir fried the Quorn "as is".

INGREDIENTS (serves 4)

Quorn Chicken Pieces (300g)
Onion (2 medium, roughly chopped)
Carrot (2 medium)
Pineapple chunks (225g tin in juice)
Bamboo shoots (225g tin)
Orange juice (400ml, smooth)
Red wine vinegar (150ml)
Soy sauce (1 tbspn, dark)
Sunflower oil (1 tbspn)
Long grain Rice (300g)

You will need two large saucepans and a sieve.

Time required: 20 minutes

1. Heat sunflower oil in large pan over a medium heat. Brown the Quorn Chicken Pieces for 3 minutes, stirring continuously.

2. Peel and cut carrot into thin strips. Add carrot and chopped onion to pan. Add pineapple chunks and juice from tin. Add bamboo shoots. Add orange juice, red wine vinegar and soy sauce. Stir thoroughly. Bring to simmering point then reduce heat, cover with lid and cook for 10 minutes. Stir occasionally.

3. Meanwhile, bring large pan of water to boil. Add rice and return to boil then cover with lid (offset to prevent boiling over). Cook for 10 minutes.

4. Drain the cooked rice.

5. Remove lid from sweet and sour mix. Cook for 2 to 3 minutes uncovered until sauce is reduced to a nice thick consistency.

6. Lightly oil a small bowl and press quarter of rice into bowl. Quickly invert onto plate and remove bowl. Repeat onto separate plates for each serving.

7. Spoon the sweet and sour mix onto the plates. Pour a little of the sauce over the rice and serve.

Calories: 573 kcal per portion

Bangers and Mash in Red Wine Gravy

Transform the kids' tea into a treat for the grown-ups. Try it with different sausages to find your favourite.

INGREDIENTS (serves 4)

Quorn Sausages (8)
Onions (2 large, roughly chopped)
Red wine (300ml)
Garlic (1 clove)
Bay leaf
Thyme (½ tspn)
Mushrooms (200g)
Sunflower oil (1 tbspn)
Black pepper
Potatoes (800g)
Margerine (25g)
Double cream (4 tbspn)

You will need two large saucepans with lids and a potato masher.

Time required: 25 minutes

1. Bring saucepan of water to boil. Peel potatoes, chop into medium-

sized chunks and add to boiling water. Cover and cook for 20 minutes.

2. Meanwhile, heat the oil over a medium-high heat in the other pan and brown the sausages, rotating them so the brown evenly all over.

3. Add the chopped onions and soften for 2 minutes, stirring frequently. frying pan over a medium high heat. Finely chop the garlic and add to the pan. Heat for 1 minute, stirring constantly.

4. Pour in the red wine and add the bay leaf and thyme and season with black pepper. As soon as pan reaches simmering point, turn the heat right down and put on the pan lid. Cook for 10 minutes.

5. Chop mushrooms and add to the pan. Add more red wine if liquid is low. Cook for a further 5 minutes.

6. Drain the potatoes. Add margarine and double cream to the pan. Using potato masher, mash the potatoes and incorporate the melted margarine and double cream to form a smooth, creamy mash.

7. Spoon potatoes onto plate. Place sausages next to potatoes and spoon the red wine gravy with the mushrooms and onions over the sausages to serve.

Calories: 626 kcal per portion

Cornish Pasty

A meal in itself. Taken down the mines by Cornish tin miners to have for their mid-day meal underground. Tasty and filling.

INGREDIENTS (makes 4 pasties, sufficient to serve 4 to 8)

Quorn Mince (300g)
Potatoes (350g)
Swede (200g)
Onions (2 large)
Beef stock cube
Black pepper
Plain flour (500g)
Margerine (150g)
Cold water (150ml)
Egg (1 medium)

You will need a mixing bowl, rolling pin and large baking tray.

Time required: 2 hours

1. Sift flour into mixing bowl. Add margarine. Mix with fork until all

margarine absorbed. Gradually add cold water and stir together until a smooth dough is formed which leaves the side of the bowl clean.

2. Turn out dough onto work surface – it should not need flouring. Knead for 5 minutes.

3. Wrap dough in clingfilm and place in refridgerator for 1 hour.

4. Meanwhile, make the filling. Finely chop the onion. Chop the potato and swede into 1cm cubes. Put Quorn mince, onion, potato and swede in clean mixing bowl. Sprinkle with crumbled beef stock cube. Mix thoroughly and season with black pepper.

5. Pre-heat oven to 175 degrees Celsius. Use margarine to grease baking tray.

6. Divide pastry in four. Roll out each into a circle approximately 20cm diameter.

7. Place quarter of the filling mix in centre of each pastry circle. Fold up two sides of pastry to meet in the middle and crimp the edges together to seal the pasty. Brush the pastry with a beaten egg.

8. Place the pasties in the middle of the pre-heated oven. Cook for 40 minutes.

9. Serve hot or allow to cool and serve cold for a picnic.

Calories: 1056 kcal per pasty, serves 1 or 2, depending on your appetite!

Cottage Pie

The classic English dinnertime staple: filling and satisfying and remarkably easy to make.

INGREDIENTS (serves 4)

Quorn Mince (300g)
Onions (2 large, roughly chopped)
Carrot (1 large)
Cinnamon (½ tspn)
Parsley (2 tspn)
Tomato purée double concentrate (1 tbspn)
Beef stock cube
Sunflower oil (1 tbspn)
Black pepper
Potatoes (800g)
Margerine (25g)
Double cream (4 tbspn)
Cheddar cheese (50g, grated)

You will need two large saucepans with lidsand a potato masher.

Time required: 50 minutes

1. Pre-heat oven to 200 degrees Celsius.

2. Bring saucepan of water to boil. Peel potatoes, chop into medium-sized chunks and add to boiling water. Cover and cook for 20 minutes.

3. Meanwhile, heat the oil over a medium heat in the other pan. Peel and chop the carrot into thin slices. Place carrot and the chopped onions in the pan and cook for 5 minutes.

4. Add the Quorn mince, cinnamon and parsley and cook for 3 minutes, stirring regularly.

5. Dissolve the beef stock cube in 300ml of boiled water. Stir in the tomato purée. Add to the mince and stir. Season with black pepper. Bring to simmering point, cover and cook for 10 minutes.

6. Drain the potatoes. Add margerine and double cream to the pan. Using potato masher, mash the potatoes and incorporate the melted margarine and double cream to form a smooth, creamy mash.

7. Spoon mince into a casserole (I like to use individual casserole dishes that can be used to serve at the table) and spread the mashed potatoes over the top. Scatter grated cheese over the potatoes. Place in the middle of the oven and bake for 20 minutes.

8. Remove and serve.

Calories: 643 kcal per portion

Full English Breakfast

Is there a more satisfying way to start the day? If so, I haven't come across it. Choose from the range of Quorn Sausages to find the taste that suits you best.

INGREDIENTS (per person)

Quorn Bacon Rashers (2)
Quorn Sausage
Egg
Mushrooms (30g approx)
Baked beans (140g approx)
Bread (1 slice)
Sunflower oil (1 tbspn)

You will need a large frying pan and spatula plus a separate saucepan for the baked beans.

Time required: 10 minutes

1. Heat the oil in the frying pan over a medium high heat. Add the sausage. Cook for 6 minutes, turning regularly to brown evenly.

2. After 2 minutes, add mushrooms. Keep them moving in the pan to

ensure they are cooked through without over-cooking anywhere.

3. After another minute place saucepan of beans over a medium heat and cook. Keep stirring and turn heat down, if necessary, to prevent beans drying out.

4. After 4th minute of cooking sausage (i.e. after another minute), crack egg into frying pan and add Quorn bacon rashers. If, like me, you prefer your eggs sunny-side-up then you can cook the yolk by tipping the pan slightly so that a pool of hot oil collects that can be spooned over the yolk. Alternatively, flip the egg after a minute to cook both sides. Flip Quorn rashers after 1 minute. Watch carefully to ensure they don't overcook – remove if necessary when cooked how you want them. I prefer mine ever so slightly crisp on around the edges.

5. All the ingredients should now be cooked to perfection and should be transferred to the plate. Cut a slice of bread in half and add to frying pan to soak up the last of the oil. Fry for 30 seconds on each side then add to the plate.

6. Serve with a freshly brewed cup of tea.

Calories: 623 kcal per portion

Lancashire Hotpot

It's so simple to make yet it tastes superb. A real pick me up on those dreary wet winter evenings.

INGREDIENTS (serves 4)

Quorn Steak Strips (400g)
Onion (2 large)
Potatoes (400g)
Beef stock cube
Worcestershire sauce (1 tspn)
Bay leaf
Thyme (½ tspn)
Black pepper
Sunflower oil (1 tbspn)
Margerine (20g)

You will need a large casserole dish with a lid.

Time required: 45 minutes

1. Pre-heat oven to 175 degrees Celsius.

2. Heat the oil over a medium high heat. Fry the onions for 3 minutes to soften them. Add the Quorn Steak Strips. Fry for further 3 minutes, stirring regularly.

3. Dissolve the beef stock cube in 500ml of hot water. Pour gradually into the casserole, stirring continuously. Add Worcestershire sauce, bay leaf and thyme. Season with Black pepper. Stir.

4. Peel the potatoes and cut into slices about 1cm thick. Layer the potato slices over the casserole mix. Cover with lid and place in middle of pre-heated oven.

5. Cook with lid on for 20 minutes. Remove lid and cook for further 10 minutes.

6. Remove casserole from oven. Dot the potatoes with margerine.

7. Grill casserole under a hot grill for 5 minutes or until potatoes turn brown. Serve when ready.

Calories: 392 kcal per portion

Quorn in Ale Pudding

The classic English comfort food that works so well. It never fails to take me back to my childhood though I'm sure that it never had Theakston's Old Peculiar in it back then.

INGREDIENTS (serves 4)

Quorn Steak Strips (200g)
Onion (2 medium)
Self-raising flour (200g)
Vegetable suet (100g)
English Ale (100ml)
Beef stock cube
Thyme (½ tspn)
Black pepper
Sunflower oil (1 tbspn)
Potatoes (400g)
Carrots (250g)
Margerine (20g)

You will need a large steamer, a medium-sized pudding basin and a mixing bowl.

Time required: 2 hours 45 minutes

1. Roughly chop the onions. Fry over a medium heat in the lower saucepan of the steamer for 2 minutes. Add the Quorn Steak Strips and cook for a further 2 minutes.

2. Add the ale and crumble the beef stock cube into the gravy. Add the thyme then stir and leave to simmer for 5 minutes.

3. Meanwhile mix the self-raising flour and suet in a bowl. Add water a little at a time and stir in. The pastry mix will form a smooth mix which leaves the sides of the bowl clean. Season with black pepper.

4. Set aside one quarter of the pastry to form the base. Roll out the pastry to form a circle about 1 cm thick. Lightly grease the pudding basin and line it with the rolled out pastry.

5. Carefully spoon the Quorn and onions in gravy into the pudding.

6. Roll out the remaining pastry mix into a circle big enough to cover the base of the pudding basin. Place it carefully over the pudding and press it in round the sides to seal the pudding. Cover the top of the pudding basin with foil, sealing it down over the sides of the basin.

7. Rinse the saucepan and fill with water to two-thirds full. Place over a high heat and bring to the boil. Lower the heat and place the steamer over the saucepan. Put the pudding basin in the steamer and cover with lid.

8. Steam the pudding for 2½ hours. Check the water level in the lower saucepan periodically to ensure it does not boil dry.

9. When there is about 25 minutes steaming time remaining, peel the carrots. Cut the potatoes and carrots into medium sized pieces and place in the lower saucepan to cook.

10. When it is ready, remove the pudding basin from the steamer. Take off the foil. Carefully, place a plate over the basin and up-end it to turn the pudding out onto the plate. It is then ready to cut and serve with the vegetables basted with margarine.

Calories: 668 kcal per portion

Toad in the Hole

Children love it and it does no harm sometimes for grown up kids to revert to their childhood. Just don't ask me where the name comes from – no wonder English is so hard to master. Be assured, no amphibians were harmed in the making of this dish.

INGREDIENTS (serves 4)

Quorn Sausages (8)
Plain flour (150g plus 1 tspn)
Eggs (2 medium)
Milk (150ml)
Water (100ml)
Black pepper
Sunflower oil (2 tbspn)
Onion (1 medium)
Beef stock cube

You will need a large mixing bowl, a frying pan and a baking tin(s).

Time required: 45 minutes

1. Preheat oven to 220 degrees Celsius. Place baking tin with tablespoon oil in oven to warm too. I like to make four individual puddings in separate tins.

2. Sift plain flour into bowl. Add egg and whisk until absorbed. Make up mixture of milk and water. Add gradually to batter, mixing continuously. Season with black pepper and set aside.

3. Heat tablespoon oil in frying pan over medium heat. Brown sausages for 2 or 3 minutes.

4. Pour the batter into the preheated baking tin(s). Place the sausages in the tin. Return to top of oven and cook for 25 minutes.

5. Shortly before the puddings are ready, chop the onion and fry in the pan over a medium heat for 2 minutes.

6. Dissolve beef stock cube in 250ml of boiled water and carefully add to frying pan. Bring to simmering point. Make up a paste of 1 teaspoon plain flour with a little cold water and pour this into the gravy, stirring continuously, to thicken it.

7. Serve puddings on plates with gravy poured over.

Calories: 420 kcal per portion

Traditional Sunday Roast with Yorkshire Pudding

Whether you serve this every week, or only on festive occasions such as Christmas or Easter, this traditional roast dinner never fails to satisfy.

INGREDIENTS (serves 4)

Quorn Family Roast
Onion (2 large, 1 small)
Potatoes (400g)
Carrots (300g)
Parsnips (300g)
Chicken stock cube
Thyme (½ tspn)
Rosemary (½ tspn)
Clear Honey (4 tspn)
Sunflower oil (2 tbspn)
Plain flour (1 tspn)

For the Yorkshire Puddings:
Plain flour (75g)
Milk (75 ml)

Water (55 ml)
Egg (1 medium)
Black pepper
Sunflower oil (1 tbspn)

For the stuffing:
Breadcrumbs (4 slices, grated)
Onion (1 large, finely chopped)
Sage (2 tspn, dried)

You will need a large roasting tin, two mixing bowls, a frying pan and a large saucepan with a lid.

Time required: 1 hour 5 minutes

1. Pre-heat oven to 220 degrees Celsius.

2. Pierce inner bag of Quorn Family Roast at a number of different spots. Place in roasting tray with 1 tablespoon of oil. Place tray in centre of pre-heated oven to cook for 55 minutes.

3. Meanwhile, sift plain flour into bowl to make Yorkshire Pudding batter. Add egg and whisk until absorbed. Make up mixture of milk and water. Add gradually to batter, mixing continuously. Season with black pepper and set aside.

4. Now make the stuffing by grating 4 slices of bread and mixing the crumbs in a bowl with one finely chopped onion. Add dried sage. Add water a little at a time and continue mixing until the stuffing comes together in a firm, moist ball.

5. Bring pan of water to boil. Peel potatoes and parboil for 5 minutes.

6. When the Quorn Family Roast has been cooking for about 25 minutes, remove potatoes from water and set that aside to make your gravy. Now remove roasting tray from oven and carefully place potatoes in tray - beware of spitting fat if there is still water on the surface of the potatoes. Carefully spoon the hot oil over the potatoes to ensure they will crisp nicely. Sprinkle the potatoes with rosemary. Return the roasting tray to the centre of the oven.

7. Pour oil into Yorkshire Pudding tin. I like to use a baking tray and make individual puddings but you can also use a large tin to make a

single Yorkshire pudding to share. Place this tray in the top of the oven to heat the oil.

8. Peel the carrots and parsnip then cut them lengthways into two or four depending on size. Baste the parsnips with the honey. Peel and cut the large onions in half.

9. When the Quorn Family Roast has been cooking for 35 minutes, remove the roasting tray from the oven. Place the honey-basted parsnips in the tray. Place the carrots in the tray and spoon oil over them, ensuring they are well coated. Sprinkle thyme over carrots. Place the onion halves in the roasting tray and spoon oil over them, ensring they are well coated. Place stuffing mix in tray. Return tray to oven to cook for 20 minutes.

10. Remove Yorkshire Pudding tin from oven. Pour batter into tin/individual moulds in baking tray. Return this tray to the top of the oven to cook for 20 minutes.

11. When the Quorn Family Roast has been cooking for 50 minutes you can start to make the gravy. Roughly chop the small onion and fry gently in a little sunflower oil over a low heat in the large frying pan for 2 minutes. Carefully add the water reserved from parboiling the potatoes. Crumble the chicken stock cube into the pan and stir until dissolved.

12. Remove the roasting tray and Yorkshire Pudding tray from the oven. Place the roasted vegetables, Yorkshire Puddings and stuffing on the plates ready to serve.

13. Pour any excess oil from the trays into the gravy to add flavour. Make up a paste of the plain flour with a little cold water and pour this into the gravy, stirring continuously, to thicken it.

14. Remove the inner bag from the Quorn Family Roast and carve. Place the slices on the plates. Pour the gravy over the roast dinner and serve.

Calories: 720 kcal per portion (with an individual Yorkshire Pudding)

Quorn Bourguignonne with Dauphinois Potatoes

Cooked in the distinctive red wine of the Burgundy region of France and served with rich, creamy potatoes, this is a hearty meal fit for a Prince.

INGREDIENTS (serves 4)

For the Bourguignonne:
Quorn Steak Strips (400g)
Onion (1 large, roughly chopped)
Burgundy red wine (500ml)
Garlic (2 cloves)
Thyme (½ tspn, dried)
Bay leaf (1)
Beef stock cube
Mushrooms (150g)
Black pepper
Sunflower oil (1 tbspn)

For the Dauphinois Potatoes
Potatoes (400g)
Garlic (1 clove)

Double Cream (200ml)
Milk (200ml)
Nutmeg
Margerine (25g)
Black pepper

You will need a large casserole dish with a lid, a shallow gratin dish and a mixing bowl.

Time required: 1 hour 10 minutes

1. Pre heat the oven to 150 degrees Celsius.

2. Peel the potatoes. Slice them thinly. Butter the gratin dish and spread a layer of potatoes over the base. Finely chop the garlic and sprinkle about half over the potato layer. Season with black pepper.

3. Add a second layer of potatoes and top with remaining garlic and black pepper. Add a top layer of potatoes. Mix the cream and milk together in a bowl and pour over the potatoes. Grate a little nutmeg over the dish.

4. Finally add a few dabs of butter over the potato layer and place the dish in the pre-heated oven on the top shelf to cook for about an hour.

5. Meanwhile, heat the oil in the casserole dish over a medium heat and soften the chopped onion for 3 minutes. Add the Quorn steak strips and continue to fry over medium heat for another 2 minutes.

6. Add the red wine and crumbled beef stock cube to the casserole dish and stir. Add the garlic, finely chopped, thyme and bay leaf. Add black pepper to taste. Stir again. Put the lid on the casserole and place that in the oven on the middle shelf.

7. After Bourguignonne casserole has been cooking for 30 minutes, remove from oven and add mushrooms (sliced if large or whole if small button mushrooms). Replace lid and return to oven for further 15 minutes.

8. Remove Bourguignonne and potatoes from oven. Extract the bay leaf and serve immediately with a glass of Red Burgundy wine.

Calories: 735 kcal per portion (Quorn Bourguignonne 352 kcal plus Dauphinois Potatoes 383 kcal) Glass of wine extra!

Quorn au Pot with Boulangère Potatoes

A French peasant stew served with the poor man's equivalent of Dauphinois potatoes though they taste just as good.

INGREDIENTS (serves 4)

Quorn Family Roast
Onion (2 large, roughly chopped)
Carrots (4 medium)
Turnip (2 small)
Dry White Wine (300ml)
Garlic (2 cloves)
Thyme (½ tspn, dried)
Parsley (½ tspn, dried)
Bay leaf (1)
Chicken stock cube
Mushrooms (200g)
Black pepper
Plain flour (1 tspn)
Sunflower oil (3 tbspn)

For the Boulangère Potatoes
Potatoes (800g)

Onion (1 medium)
Garlic (1 clove)
Milk (150ml)
Chicken stock (150ml –from stock made for casserole)
Black pepper

You will need a large casserole dish, a saucepan and a shallow gratin dish.

Time required: 1 hour 20 minutes

1. Pre heat the oven to 180 degrees Celsius.

2. Heat the oil in the casserole dish over a medium high heat. Chop the carrots into chunks about 2cm long and chop the turnips into 8 pieces. Fry the carrots and turnip for about 5 minutes then remove.

3. Turn the heat down a little and fry the onions and cruched garlic for about 3 minutes then remove.

4. Remove the Quorn Family Roast from all the packaging, including the wrapper in which it is normally roasted. Brown the surface of the Quorn Roast in the casserole, rotating it gradually so that it is browned evenly all over.

5. Now replace the carrots, turnip, onion and garlic in the casserole, surrounding the roast in the centre.

6. Dissolve the chicken stock cube in 600ml of hot water. Pour 450ml of the chicken stock into the casserole. Pour in 300ml of white wine. Add thyme, parsley and bay leaf then season with black pepper to taste. Stir the casserole to ensure the ingredients are well mixed.

7. Bring casserole up to simmering point then place in pre-heated oven on middle shelf. Cook for 30 minutes.

8. Meanwhile, peel the potatoes. Slice them thinly. Butter the gratin dish and spread a layer of potatoes over the base. Finely chop the onion and garlic and sprinkle about half over the potato layer. Season with black pepper.

9. Add a second layer of potatoes and top with remaining onion and garlic and again season with black pepper. Add a top layer of potatoes. Mix Pour the remaining 150ml of chicken stock, mixed together with the

milk, over the potatoes. Place in oven on middle shelf to cook for 45 minutes.

10. Slice the mushrooms. When the casserole has been cooking for 30 minutes, remove it from the oven, add the sliced mushrooms and stir. Return the casserole to the oven to cook for another 30 minutes.

11. Remove casserole and potatoes from the oven.

12. Pour the liquid from the casserole into a saucepan. You can also add any liquid remaining from cooking the potatoes. Heat to simmering point. Make a paste of the plain flour and a little cold water. Add to the liquid and stir continuously over a low heat until the gravy thickens nicely.

13. Slice the Quorn Roast and serve with the vegetables from the casserole and the potatoes. Pour the gravy over the Quorn Roast and the vegetables.

Calories: 633 kcal per portion (Quorn au Pot 443 kcal plus Boulangère Potatoes 190 kcal)

Quorn au Vin with Lyonnaise Potatoes

Whether it is the thick red wine sauce or the crisp potatoes cooked in the style of France's second city, this meal always satisfies.

INGREDIENTS (serves 4)

For the Quorn au Vin:
Quorn Fillets (8)
Onion (1 large, roughly chopped)
Dry red wine (500ml)
Garlic (2 cloves)
Thyme (½ tspn, dried)
Bay leaf (1)
Chicken stock cube
Mushrooms (150g)
Black pepper
Sunflower oil (1 tbspn)
Plain flour (1 tbspn)
Margerine (25g)

For the Lyonnaise Potatoes

Potatoes (400g)
Onion (1 small, finely chopped)
Black pepper
Sunflower Oil (1 tbspn)

You will need two large saucepans and a frying pan.

Time required: 50 minutes

1. Heat the oil over a high heat in a large pan. Brown the Quorn fillets, turning frequently. After 2 minutes turn the heat down to medium and add the onion and crushed garlic cloves. Soften gently for 3 minutes.

2. Add the red wine, thyme, bay leaf and crumbled stock cube and stir. Turn the heat up till the mix comes to a simmer. Reduce the heat, cover the pan with a lid and leave to simmer for 15 minutes.

3. Peel the potatoes. Parboil them for 10 minutes in a separate pan.

4. After the Quorn au Vin has been simmering for 15 minutes, add in the mushrooms. They can be left whole if they are small, otherwise slice them before adding. Recover the pan and return to simmer.

5. Pre-warm the oven to 50 degrees Celsius.

6. Now you can return to the Lyonnaise potatoes. Slice the parboiled potatoes thinly. Heat the sunflower oil in a frying pan and sauté the potato slices, turning frequently so they are cooked evenly.

7. When the potatoes are done transfer them to a warming plate covered with kitchen roll to absorb any excess oil. Place in pre-warmed oven. You may need to do this in batches.

8. In the remaining oil, fry the finely chopped onion over a low heat until it starts to turn brown. Transfer to the warming plate with the potatoes and replace in the warm oven.

9. Remove the cooked Quorn fillets, mushrooms and as much of the onion as you can from the pan and transfer it to another warming plate and place in the warmed oven.

10. Turn up the heat on the remaining red wine sauce. Mix the flour and margarine to make a paste and stir this into the sauce. Stir continuously

until it thickens.

11. Remove Quorn fillets, muchrooms, sauce onions, potatoes and fried onions from the oven. Transfer to plates (2 fillets per person). Toss the fried onions over the potatoes. Pour the thick red wine sauce over the fillets and mushrooms and sauce onions. Serve immediately.

Calories: 638 kcal per portion (Quorn au Vin 393 kcal plus Lyonnaise Potatoes 245 kcal)

Tartiflette

This dish from France's Haute Savoie region is a favourite way to fill up after a hard day's ski-ing. You can let the après-ski continue with this recipe after you get home. It is traditionally made with Reblochon cheese but I've used other soft, French cheeses with equal success.

INGREDIENTS (serves 4)

Quorn Bacon Rashers (240g)
Potatoes (800g)
Onion (2 large, roughly chopped)
Dry white wine (150ml)
Garlic (2 cloves)
Black pepper
Double cream (200ml)
Sunflower oil (1 tbspn)
Reblochon cheese (400g)

You will need a large casserole, a large saucepan and a frying pan.

Time required: 45 minutes

1. Preheat the oven to 200 degrees Celsius.

2. Peel and parboil the potatoes in a large pan of water for 8 minutes. Remove from heat.

3. Meanwhile, heat oil in frying pan over medium heat. Soften onions for 3 minutes, stirring occasionally. Add finely chopped garlic. Cut the Quorn Bacon Rashers crossways into short strips about 1.5 cm wide. Add to frying pan. Cook for 3 minutes, stirring constantly.

4. Add wine to frying pan and continue stirring until most is absorbed – about 1 to 2 minutes. Remove from heat.

5. Drain and cut potatoes into thin slices. Layer slices in base of buttered casserole – using about one third of the potatoes.

6. Spoon half Quorn and onion mix over potatoes and spread to cover. Add a second layer of potatoes. Then the remainder of the Quorn and onion mix. Finally add the last layer of the potato slices.

7. Season with plenty of black pepper then pour the cream over the casserole.

8. Cut the cheese into slices and layer over the top of the casserole. Place in oven and cook for about 25 minutes until the cheese is bubbling.

9. Remove from oven and serve immediately.

Calories: 920 kcal per portion

Moussaka

A classic aubergine based dish with cinnamon and nutmeg adding a traditional hint of spice to this Greek recipe.

INGREDIENTS (serves 4)

Quorn Mince (400g)
Aubergine (2, large)
Onion (2 large, roughly chopped)
Garlic (2 cloves)
Plum tomatoes (400g)
Tomato purée double concentrate (2 tbspn)
Dry red wine (100ml)
Cinnamon (1 tspn)
Parsley (1 tspn)
Beef stock cube
Black pepper
Margerine (75g)
Plain flour (75g)
Milk (500ml)
Egg (2 medium)

Sunflower oil (3 tbspn)
Nutmeg
Gruyère cheese (50g)

You will need a large casserole, two saucepans and a frying pan.

Time required: 1 hour 10 minutes

1. Preheat the oven to 160 degrees Celsius.

2. Heat 1 tablespoon of oil in large saucepan over medium heat. Soften onions for 3 minutes, stirring occasionally. Add finely chopped garlic. Cook for further 3 minutes, stirring occasionally.

3. Add Quorn mince. Continue to fry gently for 2 minutes.

4. Add wine, cinnamon and parsley. Crumble stock cube into pan and season with black pepper. Continue to fry gently for a further 2 minutes.

5. Add tomatoes and tomato purée. Stir. Return pan to simmering point and allow to simmer for 10 minutes.

6. Meanwhile, slice aubergines into 1cm thick rounds. Heat more oil in frying pan over medium high heat. Fry aubergines for about 1 minute on each side. You will need to do this in batches, replenishing the oil as necessary.

7. In casserole, cover base with layer of aubergines, then spoon over half the Quorn mince mixture. Now add another layer of aubergines, followed by the remainder of the mince and finally a top layer of aubergines.

8. In a fresh pan, melt the margarine over a low heat. Stir in the flour to form a thick paste. Gradually add milk, stirring constantly until you have a smooth, creamy sauce. Season with a little black pepper and grated nutmeg.

9. Grate the cheese and add to the sauce. Whisk the eggs and pour into the sauce mix. Stir until fully incorporated into sauce.

10. Pour sauce over aubergines and Quorn mince in casserole. Place casserole in pre-heated oven and cook for 40 minutes.

11. Remove from oven and serve immediately.

Calories: 642 kcal per portion

Hungarian Goulash

A spicy treat from the heart of Europe. One to dish up on a cold Winter evening to revive your spirits.

INGREDIENTS (serves 4)

Quorn Steak Strips (400g)
Onion (2 large)
Garlic (1 clove)
Paprika (1 tbspn)
Beef stock cube
Plum Tomatoes (400g)
Red pepper (1 large)
Soured Cream (150ml)
Black Pepper
Sunflower Oil (1 tbspn)
Long Grain Rice (300g)

You will need two large saucepans and a sieve.

Time required: 45 minutes

1. Heat the oil in a pan over a medium heat. Roughly chop the onion and add to the pan to soften gently for 5 minutes. Finely chop the garlic and add to the pan for the last 2 minutes.

2. Turn up heat. Add the steak strips and cook for 2 minutes, stirring constantly.

3. Add the paprika and crumbled beef stock cube. Stir in. Add the tomatoes and season with black pepper. Stir thoroughly and cover pan with lid. Cook for 10 minutes.

4. Chop the red pepper and add to the goulash mix. Cook for 10 minutes.

5. Bring large pan of water to boil. Add rice and stir. Stir once and return to boil then cover with lid (offset to prevent boiling over). Cook for 10 minutes.

6. Drain cooked rice in sieve and spoon onto plates to form rings.

7. Add soured cream to goulash mix and stir until creamy (30 seconds). Spoon goulash into the rice rings and serve immediately with a sprinkling of paprika to decorate.

Calories: 733 kcal per portion

Paprika Quorn Fillets

A characteristic Hungarian dish with a little extra kick from the cayenne pepper.

INGREDIENTS (serves 4)

Quorn Chicken Fillets (8)
Onion (2 large)
Paprika (1 tbspn)
Cayenne pepper (1 tspn)
Chicken stock cube
Plum Tomatoes (400g)
Plain flour (2 tspn)
Green pepper (1 large)
Soured Cream (150ml)
Black Pepper
Sunflower Oil (1 tbspn)
Tagliatelle (300g)

You will need a large casserole with a lid and a saucepan.

Time required: 1 hour

1. Pre-heat the oven to 150 degrees Celsius.

2. Heat the oil in a casserole over a medium heat. Brown the Quorn Chicken Fillets for 5 minutes.

3. Roughly chop the onion and add to the pan to soften gently for 5 minutes.

4. Add the cayenne pepper and paprika. Season with black pepper. Stir to ensure the fillets are well coated with the spices. Add flour and stir again.

5. Add plum tomatoes and chop with knife in pan. Stir. Dissolve the chicken stock cube in 150ml of hot water and add to the pan. Stir thoroughly.

6. Bring to simmering point and allow to simmer for 10 minutes.

7. Chop green pepper and add to mix. Stir. Cover with casserole lid and place in pre-heated oven to cook for 30 minutes.

8. When there is 10 minutes cooking time remaining for the paprika fillets, place 300g of tagliatelle in a pan of boiling water. Cover with lid (offset to prevent boiling over). Cook for 10 minutes.

9. Drain tagliatelle and serve onto plates.

10. Remove casserole from oven. Transfer the Quorn fillets to the plates. Add soured cream to the paprika sauce and stir in so that it is incorporated but retains the marble effect. Spoon over the Quorn fillets. Sprinkle with paprika to decorate and serve.

Calories: 708 kcal per portion

Quorn Biryani

A great way to enjoy those Indian flavours that is quick and easy to prepare. I've made this with Quorn Chicken Pieces but you could try it with Quorn Steak Strips which works just as well.

INGREDIENTS (serves 4)

Quorn Chicken Pieces (400g)
Onion (2 large)
Garlic (4 clove)
Ginger (5cm root, grated or 1 tspn powder)
Coriander (2 tspn, ground)
Chilli powder (1 tspn)
Cumin (1 tspn)
Turmeric (½ tspn)
Cinnamon (½ tspn)
Nutmeg
Yoghurt (200ml)
Sunflower Oil (2 tbspn)
Basmati Rice (300g)

You will need a large frying pan with a lid, a large saucepan and a sieve.

Time required: 25 minutes

1. Bring a large pan of water to the boil. Add the Basmati rice. Stir once and return to boil then cover with lid (offset to prevent boiling over) and turn the heat down low. Cook for 10 minutes.

2. Meanwhile, heat the oil in the frying pan over a low heat. Roughly chop the onion. Finely chop the garlic. Add the onion, garlic and ginger and fry gently for 5 minutes, stirring regularly.

3. Add the Quorn Chicken Pieces and continue to cook for 5 minutes, stirring regularly.

4. Add the ground coriander, chilli, cumin, turmeric, cinnamon and a small grating of nutmeg to the pan and continue to fry gently for further 2 minutes, stirring regularly.

5. Add the yoghurt and bring to simmer for 2 minutes.

6. Drain the rice in the sieve. Add rice to the biryani mix. Cover frying pan with lid and cook gently for 5 minutes.

7. Spoon onto plates and serve immediately.

Calories: 468 kcal per portion

Quorn Korma with Pilau Rice and Naan Bread

A delicious aromatic, creamy Indian dish. I've made this with Quorn Chicken Pieces but you could try it with Quorn Steak Strips and use a beef stock cube for the pilau rice and it works just as well.

INGREDIENTS (serves 4)

Quorn Chicken Pieces (400g)
Onion (2 large)
Garlic (4 clove)
Ginger (5cm root, grated or 1 tspn powder)
Cardomam pods (12)
Coriander (1 tspn, ground)
Chilli powder (½ tspn)
Cumin (1 tspn)
Turmeric (½ tspn)
Cloves (4)
Bay leaf
Plain flour (25g)
Saffron (1 pinch)

Yoghurt (50ml)
Black pepper
Double Cream (75ml)
Chicken stock cube
Sunflower Oil (2 tbspn)
Basmati Rice (300g)
Coriander leaves (1 tspn)

For the Naan bread:
Strong white flour (500g)
Dried Yeast (2 tspn)
Fennel seeds (2 tspn)
Bicarbonate of Soda (½ tspn)
Salt (½ tspn)
Egg (1, medium)
Olive Oil (2 tspn)
Yoghurt (200ml)
Milk (300ml)

You will need a large frying pan, a large saucepan, a bowl, a baking tray, a rolling pin and a sieve.

Time required: 1 hour 5 minutes plus 8 hours for Quorn Chicken Pieces to marinade in yoghurt

1. Place the Quorn Chicken Pieces in a non-metallic bowl. Season with black pepper and spoon 50ml of yoghurt over them. Mix thoroughly so the pieces are coated in yoghurt and place in refridgerator for 8 hours to marinade.

2. Pre-heat the oven to 50 degrees Celsius.

3. Start by making the dough for the naan bread. Mix the flour, yeast, salt, bicarbonate of soda and fennel seeds together in the bowl. Add the egg, olive oil and yoghurt. Mix thoroughly.

4. Warm the milk in a pan or microwave until it is hand hot. Gradually add the milk to the dough, stirring constantly. Stop adding the milk when the dough as smooth and the bowl comes clean as you stir.

5. On a floured work-surface, knead the dough for 6 to 8 minutes until smooth and elastic.

6. Return the dough to the bowl and place it on the middle shelf of the warm oven to rise. This will take about 30 to 40 minutes. It should double in size.

7. Meanwhile, heat the oil in the frying pan over a low heat. Roughly chop the onion. Finely chop the garlic. Add the onion, garlic and ginger and fry gently for 5 minutes, stirring regularly.

8. Crush the seeds of the cardomam pods. Separate the head of the cloves from the stalk. Add the crushed cardomam seeds, ground coriander, chilli, cumin, turmeric, cloves and bay leaf to the pan and continue to fry gently for further 5 minutes, stirring regularly.

9. Add flour and saffron Gradually add 300ml of cold water into the pan, stirring continuously. Bring up to simmering point. Cover and leave to cook for 10 minutes.

10. Dissolve the chicken stock cube in a large pan of water and bring it to the boil. Add the Basmati rice. Stir once and return to boil then cover with lid (offset to prevent boiling over). Cook for 10 minutes.

11. Add the Quorn Chicken Pieces coated in yoghurt to the korma mix. Add double cream. Bring back to simmering point. Allow to simmer for 10 minutes.

12. Meanwhile take the risen dough and divide it into 8 portions. Roll out each portion on a floured work-surface into the traditional triangular shape.

13. Heat the grill to very hot and bake the naan breads on a tray allowing 1 minute per side, turning the breads halfway through. Unless you have a very large grill, you will probably need to do this in batches, in which case, keep the cooked naans warm in the oven.

14. Drain the rice in the sieve. Spoon drained rice and korma mix onto plates. Garnish with coriander leaves. Serve with the naan breads. (The recipe makes enough for two naan breads each but I find one is plenty – so you can freeze four of the naans for the next time if you like.)

Calories: 639 kcal per portion, naan breads 350 kcal each

Quorn Madras with Bombay Potatoes

A strong curry from the south of India combined with potatoes in a style from the north west coastal city. I've used Quorn Steak Strips but you could try it with Quorn Chicken Pieces and use a chicken stock cube for a variation on this recipe.

INGREDIENTS (serves 4)

Quorn Steak Strips (400g)
Onion (2 large)
Garlic (2 clove)
Ginger (5cm root, grated or 1 tspn powder)
Chilli powder (2½ tspn)
Cumin (1 tspn)
Turmeric (1½ tspn)
Garam Masala (1 tspn)
Mustard powder (1½ tspn)
Tomatoes (450g)
Tomato purée double concentrate (2 tbspn)
Red lentils (200g)
Beef stock cube

Potatoes (800g)
Sunflower Oil (4 tbspn)
Coriander leaves (2 tspn)

You will need two large saucepans.

Time required: 45 minutes

1. Heat 2 tablespoons of oil in the frying pan over a low heat. Roughly chop the onion. Finely chop the garlic. Add the onion, garlic, ginger, 1 teaspoon of the chilli powder, cumin, 1 teaspoon of the turmeric, garam masala and 1 teaspoon of the mustard. Fry gently for 5 minutes, stirring regularly.

2. Add the Quorn Steak Strips and continue frying for a further 5 minutes, stirring continuously.

3. Chop the tomatoes. Add the tomatoes and tomato purée to the pan. Stir the mix. Dissolve the beef stock cube in 500ml of hot water. Pour the stock over the mix. Add red lentils and stir. Bring to simmering point. Cover and leave to cook for 15 minutes, stirring occasionally to prevent the mix sticking to the bottom of the pan. Add a little extra stock if needed.

4. Meanwhile, chop the potatoes into cubes approximately 2cm wide. In a separate pan, cook for 8 minutes in boiling water.

5. Drain the potatoes. Add the remaining 2 tablespoons of oil and return to hob over a medium high heat. Add the remaining ½ teaspoon of chilli powder, ½ teaspoon of turmeric and ½ teaspoon of mustard powder. Cook for further 5 minutes. Stir regularly to ensure potatoes covered with spices.

6. Stir coriander leaves into Madras mix and allow to cook for 1 minute.

7. Serve Madras mix and Bombay potatoes, garnished with more coriander leaves, side by side on plates. Have a bottle of good quality Indian beer to hand for the authentic experience.

Calories: 740 kcal per portion. Beer extra!

Quorn Tikka Masala with Rice and Naan Bread

An Indian mainstay. This works just as well if you make it with Quorn Steak Strips.

INGREDIENTS (serves 4)

Quorn Chicken Pieces (400g)
Onion (2 large)
Garlic (2 clove)
Ginger (5cm root, grated or 1 tspn powder)
Coriander (1 tspn, ground)
Chilli powder (2 tspn)
Cumin (1tspn)
Turmeric (1 tspn)
Tomato purée double concentrate (4 tbspns)
Tomatoes (2 large)
Yoghurt (100ml)
Double Cream (100ml)
Lime juice (10ml)
Chicken stock cube
Sunflower Oil (2 tbspn)

Basmati Rice (300g)
Coriander leaves (1 tspn)

For the Naan bread:
Strong white flour (500g)
Dried Yeast (2 tspn)
Fennel seeds (2 tspn)
Bicarbonate of Soda (½ tspn)
Salt (½ tspn)
Egg (1, medium)
Olive Oil (2 tspn)
Yoghurt (200ml)
Milk (300ml)

You will need a large frying pan, a large saucepan, a mixing bowl, a baking tray, a rolling pin and a sieve.

Time required: 1 hour 10 minutes

1. Pre-heat the oven to 50 degrees Celsius.

2. Start by making the dough for the naan bread. Mix the flour, yeast, salt, bicarbonate of soda and fennel seeds together in the bowl. Add the egg, olive oil and yoghurt. Mix thoroughly.

3. Warm the milk in a pan or microwave until it is hand hot. Gradually add the milk to the dough, stirring constantly. Stop adding the milk when the dough as smooth and the bowl comes clean as you stir.

4. On a floured work-surface, knead the dough for 6 to 8 minutes until smooth and elastic.

5. Return the dough to the bowl and place it on the middle shelf of the warm oven to rise. This will take about 30 to 40 minutes. It should double in size.

6. Meanwhile, heat the oil in the frying pan over a medium-high heat. Roughly chop the onion. Finely chop the garlic. Add the onion, garlic and Quorn Chicken pieces to the pan. Fry for 1 minute.

7. Add the ginger, ground coriander, chilli, cumin and turmeric to the pan and add continue to fry for further 2 minutes.

8. Chop the tomatoes. Add tomatoes and tomato purée to the pan. Continue cooking for 5 minutes. Remove from the heat and allow to cool a little.

9. Dissolve a large pan of water and bring it to the boil. Add the Basmati rice. Stir once and return to boil then cover with lid (offset to prevent boiling over). Cook for 10 minutes.

10. Add the yoghurt and double cream to the tikka masala mix and return to the heat. Bring to simmering point. Add lime juice. Reduce heat and allow to simmer for 10 minutes.

11. Meanwhile take the risen dough and divide it into 8 portions. Roll out each portion on a floured work-surface into the traditional triangular shape.

12. Heat the grill to very hot and bake the naan breads on a tray allowing 1 minute per side, turning the breads halfway through. Unless you have a very large grill, you will probably need to do this in batches, in which case, keep the cooked naans warm in the oven.

13. Drain the rice in the sieve. Spoon drained rice and tikka masala onto plates. Garnish with coriander leaves. Serve with the naan breads. (The recipe makes enough for two naan breads each but I find one is plenty – so you can freeze four of the naans for the next time if you like.)

Calories: 664 kcal per portion, naan breads 350 kcal each

Quorn Vindaloo

A hot Indian curry. I've made it here with Quorn Steak Strips but, like the others, it works just as well if you make it with Quorn Chicken Pieces.

INGREDIENTS (serves 4)

Quorn Steak Strips (400g)
Red wine vinegar (100ml)
Onion (3 large)
Garlic (4 clove, finely chopped)
Ginger (5cm root, grated or 1 tspn powder)
Coriander (1 tspn, ground)
Chilli powder (4 tspn)
Mustard Powder (2 tspn)
Cumin (2 tspn)
Turmeric (2 tspn)
Paprika (2 tspn)
Cayenne Pepper (2 tspn)
Cinnamon (1 tspn)
Bay leaf (2)
Salt (1 tspn)

Yoghurt (100ml)
Sunflower Oil (6 tbspn)

You will need a large casserole with a lid and a mixing bowl.

Time required: 55 minutes plus 8 hours to marinade

1. Mix the red wine vinegar, 2 tablespoons of sunflower oil and the salt in a bowl to make the marinade. Place the Quorn Steak Strips in the marinade, ensuring they are all covered, and put in the fridge to marinade for 8 hours.

2. Pre-heat the oven to 50 degrees Celsius.

3. Heat the 2 more tablespoons of oil in a casserole over a medium heat. Roughly chop the onions and soften them in the pan for 5 minutes, stirring occasionally.

4. Add the chopped garlic, ginger, ground coriander, chilli powder, mustard powder, cumin, turmeric, paprika, cayenne pepper and cinnamon. onions and stir in. Cook for 5 minutes.

5. Add remaining 2 tablespoons of oil to casserole. Remove Quorn Steak Strips from marinade and add to casserole. Cook for 2 minutes.

6. Now add marinade to casserole and 500ml of hot water. Add bay leaves. Turn heat up and bring to simmering point.

7. Cover with lid and place in preheated oven. Cook for 10 minutes.

8. Add potatoes to casserole. Recover with lid and cook for further 25 minutes.

9. Remove from oven and serve with topping of yoghurt.

Calories: 418 kcal per portion

Tandoori Quorn with Saffron Rice

A classic Indian method of cooking in a hot clay oven that you can reproduce at home.

INGREDIENTS (serves 4)

Quorn Fillets (8)
Yoghurt (400ml)
Onion (1 small, finely chopped)
Garlic (1 clove, finely chopped)
Ginger (5cm root, grated or 1 tspn powder)
Chilli powder (1 tspn)
Garam masala (1 tspn)
Lemon Juice (20ml)
Basmati rice (300g)
Saffron

You will need a large saucepan, a mixing bowl, a baking tray and a sieve.

Time required: 40 minutes plus 8 hours to marinade

1. Place the Quorn fillets on the baking tray and pour lemon juice over them.
2. Mix the yoghurt, finely chopped onions and garlic, ginger, chilli powder and garam masala in a bowl. Spread the resulting marinade over the Quorn fillets. Place in fridge for at least 8 hours.
3. Preheat the oven to 225 degrees Celsius.
4. red wine vinegar, 2 tablespoons of sunflower oil and the salt in a bowl to make the marinade. Place the Quorn Steak Strips in the marinade, ensuring they are all covered, and put in the fridge to marinade for 8 hours.
5. Pre-heat the oven to 50 degrees Celsius.
6. Put a pinch of saffron in a large pan of water and bring it to the boil. Add the Basmati rice. Stir once and return to boil then cover with lid (offset to prevent boiling over). Cook for 10 minutes.
7. Meanwhile remove the baking tray from the fridge and brush the excess marinade from the Quorn fillets. Place on upper shelf in preheated oven. Cook for 10 minutes.
8. Drain the saffron rice in the sieve. Spoon drained rice onto plates and serve two fillets per person on the bed of rice.

Calories: 355 kcal per portion

Irish Stew and Dumplings

A filling stew, based on a traditional Irish recipe, that will satisfy all the family. Served with dumplings which always go down well with the kids – young or old.

INGREDIENTS (serves 4)

Quorn Steak Strips (400g)
Potatoes (400g)
Onion (4 large)
Carrot (300g)
Turnip (2 small)
Pearl barley (1 tbspn)
Beef stock cube
Black pepper
Self raising flour (120g)
Vegetable suet (50g)
Parsley (1 tspn)

You will need a large saucepan and a mixing bowl.

Time required: 1 hour 20 minutes

1. Peel the potatoes and cut into large chunks. Cut the onions in quarters.

Peel the carrots and cut into thick slices. Peel the turnips and cut into quarters.

2. Place a layer of the vegetables in the bottom of the pan. Then add about half the Quorn Steak Strips. Add another layer of vegetables. Then the rest of the Quorn Steak Strips. Top off with a final layer of vegetables. Add the pearl barley. Season with black pepper.

3. Dissolve the beef stock cube in a litre of boiling water. Pour over the ingredients in the pan.

4. Bring to simmering point over a medium heat then put the lid on the pan, turn down the heat and leave to simmer for 50 minutes.

5. Now mix the self raising flour, vegetable suet and dried parsley in a bowl. Season with black pepper. Add water a little at a time and mix to form a dough that sticks together and comes clear of the bowl.

6. Divide the dough into eight and roll into balls. Pop them in the top of the pan so they are almost covered by the liquid. Top up the liquid with more boiling stock if there is insufficient.

7. Recover and cook for 20 minutes. The stew is then ready to serve onto plates with extra gravy spooned over the top.

Calories: 540 kcal per portion

Italian Casserole with Risotto alla Milanese

This traditional casserole from the north of Italy is perfect with a risotto prepared in the Milanese way.

INGREDIENTS (serves 4)

For the casserole:
Quorn fillets (8)
Onion (2 large, roughly chopped)
Garlic (1 clove, finely chopped)
Dry white wine (300ml)
Tomatoes (400g)
Tomato purée double concentrate (2 tbspns)
Black pepper
Sunflower oil (1 tbspn)

For the risotto:
Arborio rice (300g)
Saffron (1 pinch)
Dry white wine (150ml)
Chicken stock cube

Sunflower oil (1 tbspn)
Onion (1 medium, finely chopped)
Parmesan cheese (50g, grated)
Black pepper

For the gremolata garnish:
Garlic (1 clove, finely chopped)
Parsley (2 tspn)

You will need a large casserole with a lid and a large saucepan.

Time required: 30 minutes

1. Heat the sunflower oil in the casserole over a medium high heat and brown the Quorn fillets on both sides for about 3 minutes. Remove fillets.

2. Turn the heat down and soften the chopped onion and chopped garlic for 2 minutes.

3. Chop the tomatoes and add to the casserole. Add white wine and tomato purée. Stir thoroughly. Bring to simmering point. Return the Quorn fillets to the casserole. Season with black pepper. Turn heat down low, cover with lid and cook for 15 minutes, stirring occasionally.

4. Meanwhile, prepare the risotto. Heat sunflower oil in saucepan over medium heat. Add saffron and chopped onion. Cook for 2 minutes.

5. Add rice and cook for 1 minute, stirring to mix thoroughly. Add white wine and stir. Bring to simmering point and cook for 5 minutes.

6. Dissolve chicken stock cube in 1 litre of boiling water. Gradually add stock as required to the rice to keep the risotto moist. Stir regularly to prevent rice sticking to the bottom of the pan.

7. After about 5 minutes, when the rice is cooked, remove from the heat. Grate the Parmesan cheese and stir into risotto. Season with black pepper.

8. Serve casserole and risotto on plates garnished with finely chopped garlic clove and parsley.

Calories: 746 kcal per portion

Lasagna al Forno

Why Italian men stay tied to Mama's apron strings. Try it with Lasagne Verde (made with spinach pasta) for a subtly different taste.

INGREDIENTS (serves 4)

For the Bolognese mix:
Quorn mince (250g)
Onion (1 large)
Garlic (2 cloves, crushed)
Plum tomatoes (200g, chopped)
Tomato purée double concentrate (2 tbspns)
Sunflower oil (1 tbspn)
Red wine (100ml)
Basil (1 tspn, dried)
Beef stock cube
Black pepper

For the cream sauce:
Milk (700ml)
Margerine (75g)

Plain flour (50g)
Double cream (100ml)
Nutmeg

Lasagna (8 sheets, dried)
Parmesan cheese (50g, grated)

You will need three large saucepans, a large bowl, a casserole dish approximately 15cm x 25cm (or you can use four individual casserole dishes if you prefer), a balloon whisk and a colander.

Time required: 1 hour

1. Finely chop the onion. Heat the oil in a pan over a low heat and gently soften the onion for 1 minute. Add the crushed garlic and continue heating for further 2 minutes, stirring continuously.

2. Turn up heat. Add Quorn mince, red wine and crumbled beef stock cube. After 1 minute add tomatoes, basil and black pepper and stir. As soon as mixture starts to bubble nicely, turn heat down to medium-low, then cover the pan. Leave to simmer gently for 15 minutes then remove from heat.

3. Bring a large pan of water to the boil and add the lasagna sheets two at a time. Cook for 4 minutes each. Remove lasagna and place in bowl of cold water to prevent them sticking to each other.

4. Turn oven on to 180 degrees Celsius.

5. In a clean pan over a medium heat, add milk, margerine and flour. Mix continuously with a balloon whisk. The sauce will gradually thicken as it reaches simmering point. Reduce heat to very low and continue to cook gently for 5 minutes.

6. Add cream to sauce and grate in a little nutmeg and a little black pepper. Stir into sauce.

7. Drain the lasagna in a colander.

8. Butter the casserole and cover base with about half the Bolognese mix. Pour over about one third of the cream sauce. Arrange 4 sheets of lasagna over the sauce.

9. Repeat with a second layer each of the remainder of the Bolognese mix, half the remaining cream sauce and the last 4 sheets of lasagna.

10. Add a final layer of the remaining cream sauce then grate the parmesan over the top.

11. Place the casserole on the middle shelf of the pre-heated oven and cook for 30 minutes.

12. Remove from the oven and serve immediately.

Calories: 743 kcal per portion

Quorn Risotto

A light and tasty variation on the classic Italian risotto made with tomatoes roasted in olive oil and balsamic vinegar.

INGREDIENTS (serves 4)

Quorn Chicken Pieces (300g)
Onion (1 large)
Garlic (2 cloves, crushed)
Baby vine tomatoes (16)
Arborio rice (300g)
Sunflower oil (1 tbspn)
Dry white wine (150ml)
Oregano (3 tspn, dried)
Chicken stock cube
Peas (150g)
Balsamic Vinegar (1 tbspn)
Olive Oil (1 tbspn)
Sunflower Oil (1 tbspn)
Black pepper
Parmesan cheese (50g)

You will need a large frying pan with a lid and a roasting tray.

Time required: 35 minutes

1. Pre-heat oven on to 180 degrees Celsius.

2. Place tomatoes on roasting tray and drizzle with the olive oil and balsamic vinegar. Scatter 1 teaspoon of oregano over the tomatoes and season with black pepper. Place on middle shelf of oven and cook for 20 minutes.

3. Meanwhile, finely chop the onion. Heat the sunflower oil in a pan over a low heat and gently soften the onion for 1 minute. Add the crushed garlic and 2 teaspoons of oregano. Continue heating for further 2 minutes, stirring continuously.

4. Turn up heat. Add Quorn Chicken Pieces. Season with black pepper and brown for 2 minutes, stirring occasionally.

5. Add Arborio rice and continue cooking for 2 minutes, stirring regularly. Add wine and bring to simmer, stirring continuously.

6. Make up 1 litre of chicken stock and pour half into pan. Stir once then cover with lid and leave to simmer for 5 minutes.

7. Add peas and remainder of stock. Stir once and recover. Leave to simmer for 10 minutes. Uncover and allow any remaining liquid to be absorbed. Remove from heat.

8. Remove tomatoes from oven and add to risotto mix together with any remaining olive oil and balsamic vinegar. Grate parmesan cheese over risotto. Stir in and serve.

Calories: 670 kcal per portion

Spaghetti Bolognese

The archetypal Italian pasta. Simple yet delicious, this humble recipe is meatier than many – if that's not a paradox for a vegetarian version.

INGREDIENTS (serves 4)

Quorn mince (250g)
Onion (1 large)
Garlic (2 cloves, crushed)
Plum tomatoes (200g, chopped)
Tomato purée double concentrate (2 tbspns)
Sunflower oil (1 tbspn)
Red wine (100ml)
Basil (1 tspn, dried)
Beef stock cube
Black pepper
Spaghetti (300g)
Parmesan cheese (50g, coarsely grated)

You will need two large saucepans and a sieve.

Time required: 20 minutes

1. Finely chop the onion. Heat the oil in a pan over a low heat and gently soften the onion for 1 minute. Add the crushed garlic and continue heating for further 2 minutes, stirring continuously.

2. Turn up heat. Add Quorn mince, red wine and crumbled beef stock cube. After 1 minute add tomatoes, basil and black pepper and stir. As soon as mixture starts to bubble nicely, turn heat down to medium-low, then cover the pan. Leave to simmer gently.

3. Bring a large pan of water to the boil and add the spaghetti. Cook for 8 to 10 minutes until the spaghetti is cooked through but still firm to bite (al dente).

4. Drain spaghetti in sieve and turn onto plates. Spoon the Bolognese sauce over the pasta and top off with coarsely grated parmesan.

Calories: 605 kcal per portion

Tagliatelle Carbonara

A taste of Italy that is quick and easy to make but with a sophisticated twist if you are entertaining.

INGREDIENTS (serves 4)

Quorn Bacon Rashers (16 rashers)
Tagliatelle (300g)
Eggs (8 medium)
Parmesan cheese (20g grated)
Garlic (4 cloves)
Sunflower oil (1 tbspn)
Black pepper

You will need a mixing bowl, a large saucepan, a frying pan and a colander.

Time required: 15 minutes

1. Half fill the saucepan with water and bring to the boil over a high heat. Add the tagliatelle and bring back to the boil. Cook for 10 minutes or until 'al dente' – firm to bite into.

2. Heat oil in frying pan over medium high heat. Cut the bacon rashers crossways to make small strips. Crush garlic. Add rashers and garlic to frying pan. Fry until rashers just begin to turn crisp (about 1½ minutes), turning frequently. Remove from heat.

3. Beat eggs in bowl. Add half the grated parmesan. Add milled black pepper to taste. Mix thoroughly.

4. When tagliatelle is cooked, drain in colander and return to saucepan. Turn heat to very low. Add egg mix and garlic bacon. Stir until tagliatelle is well coated with the egg mix.

5. Serve immediately the egg mix has cooked from the pasta's heat. Top off with remainder of grated parmesan.

Calories: 541 kcal per portion

Chilli con Quorn with Guacamole

The flavour of Mexico. You can make your own guacamole for the truly authentic taste.

INGREDIENTS (serves 4)

For the chilli:
Quorn mince (400g)
Red kidney beans (200g, dried)
Onions (2 medium)
Garlic (2 cloves)
Tomato purée double concentrate (2 tbspns)
Beef stock cube
Hot water (600ml)
Chilli powder (2 tspn)
Red pepper (1 large)
Black pepper
Sunflower oil (1 tbspn)

For the guacamole:
Tomato (1 large)

Avocado (1 medium)
Lemon juice
Onion (small, finely chopped)
Garlic (1 clove)
Chilli powder (½ tspn)
Tabasco sauce
Black pepper

Long grain rice (300g)
Soured cream (4 tbspns) to serve

You will need a mixing bowl, two large saucepans, a large casserole with a lid, a potato masher and a sieve.

Time required: 1 hour 10 minutes (plus overnight soak for the beans!)

1. Leave the dried kidney beans to soak in a pan of cold water overnight.

2. Preheat oven to 150 degrees Celsius. Replace the water in the pan of beans and bring to boil. Keep them over a medium high heat for 10 minutes.

3. Heat oil in casserole over medium heat. Chop onions and garlic and soften in casserole for 5 minutes. Add Quorn mince and stir.

4. Dissolve beef stock cube in hot water and mix in tomato purée. Pour over ingredients in casserole. Sprinkle 2 teaspoons of chilli powder into mix and stir thoroughly.

5. Add beans and stir again. Place lid on casserole and put into middle of preheated oven. Leave to cook for 20 minutes.

6. Now for the guacamole. Place tomato in a heat proof container and cover with boiling water. After a few minutes you should find it easy to make a small incision in the tomato and peel away the skin. Cut tomato in half and scoop out the seeds with a teaspoon. Chop the tomato flesh into small pieces.

7. Cut the avocado in half. Remove the stone and scoop out the flesh into a bowl. Sprinkle with lemon juice to prevent browning. Mash the avocado with a potato masher.

8. Add chopped tomato to bowl. Add finely chopped onion and crushed

garlic. Mix thoroughly. Add black pepper, ½ teaspoon of chilli powder and a few drops of Tabasco sauce to the mix. Stir thoroughly. Put guacamole in refridgerator to chill until needed.

9. Chop red pepper and add to casserole. Stir. Replace lid and return to oven for further 20 minutes.

10. Bring large pan of water to boil. Add rice and stir. Stir once and return to boil then cover with lid (offset to prevent boiling over). Cook for 10 minutes.

11. Drain cooked rice in sieve and spoon onto plates to form rings.

12. Remove casserole from oven. Spoon chilli mix into centre of rice rings. Top off the chilli with a spoon of the guacamole and a spoon of soured cream to serve.

Calories: Chilli 595 kcal per portion plus guacamole 130 kcal and soured cream 50 kcal per portion

Mole Quorn

Chocolate and chilli – it's so wrong it just has to be right. This was possibly my favourite meal ever in a small restaurant in San Cristobal de las Casas in southern Mexico.

INGREDIENTS (serves 4)

Quorn fillets (8)
Onions (2 medium, roughly chopped)
Bird's eye chillis (2)
Garlic (3 cloves, finely chopped)
Cumin (2 tspns)
Cinnamon (1 ½ tspns)
Plum tomatoes (400g)
Peanut butter (2 tbspns)
Chocolate (50g, dark – 70% cocoa solids)
Coriander leaves (2 tspns)
Sunflower oil (1 tbspn)
Long grain rice (300g)

You will need two large saucepans and a sieve.

Time required: 1 hour 10 minutes

1. Heat oil in large pan over a high heat and brown the Quorn fillets for 2 minutes on each side. Remove from pan.

2. Turn down the heat and soften the chopped onions for 2 minutes. Add the cumin, cinnamon and chopped bird's eye chillis. Cook for 2 minutes, stirring to mix thoroughly with the onions.

3. Add finely chopped garlic, peanut butter and tomatoes. Add 400ml of hot water and bring to simmering point, stirring constantly. Add Quorn fillets. Cover with lid and leave to simmer for 40 minutes.

4. Break chocolate into small pieces and add to the mole sauce. Stir until chocolate melts. Add more water if it is too thick. Leave to simmer uncovered for further 15 minutes.

5. Meanwhile bring large pan of water to boil. Add rice and stir. Stir once and return to boil then cover with lid (offset to prevent boiling over). Cook for 10 minutes.

6. Drain cooked rice in sieve and spoon onto plates.

7. Remove Quorn fillets from sauce and place on plates. Pour the sauce over the fillets. Sprinkle coriander leaves over dish to garnish.

Calories: 631 kcal per portion

Quorn Fajitas

I love the sizzle and the smell of fajitas as they cook. And it's so easy to make the tortillas, though I do cheat and roll them out on a board rather spinning and flattening them by hand the way they do in Mexico.

INGREDIENTS (serves 4)

For the stir fry:
Quorn Fillets (8)
Onions (2 medium)
Green or Red peppers (2 large)
Paprika (1 tspn)
Cumin (½ tspn)
Lime juice (20ml)
Black pepper
Sunflower oil (2 tbspn)

For the guacamole:
Tomato (1 large)
Avocado (1 medium)

Lemon juice
Onion (small, finely chopped)
Garlic (1 clove)
Chilli powder (½ tspn)
Tabasco sauce
Black pepper

For the salsa:
Plum tomatoes (400g)
Chilli powder (1 tspn)
Coriander leaves (1 tspn)
Lime juice (20ml)
Sunflower oil (1 tbspn)
Black pepper

For the tortillas:
Plain flour (200g)
Water (125ml)
Sunflower oil (1 tbspn)
Salt

Chedder cheese (200g, grated)
Soured cream (4 tbspns) to serve

You will need four mixing bowls, a large frying pan and a potato masher..

Time required: 30 minutes (plus 3 hours marinade for stir fry mix)

1. Cut the Quorn fillets into small strips. Roughly chop the onions. Cut the green or red peppers in half. De-seed and cut the peppers lengthways to create strips of about the same size as the Quorn fillet strips.

2. Place the Quorn fillet strips, onions and peppers in a bowl. Add paprika and cumin. Mix together. Add lime juice and 1 tablespoon of oil. Mix until all are covered in marinade. Season and place in refridgerator for 3 hours to absorb the flavours.

3. Now for the guacamole. Place tomato in a heat proof container and cover with boiling water. After a few minutes you should find it easy to make a small incision in the tomato and peel away the skin. Cut tomato in half and scoop out the seeds with a teaspoon. Chop the tomato flesh into small pieces.

4. Cut the avocado in half. Remove the stone and scoop out the flesh into a bowl. Sprinkle with lemon juice to prevent browning. Mash the avocado with a potato masher.

5. Add chopped tomato to bowl. Add finely chopped onion and crushed garlic. Mix thoroughly. Add black pepper, ½ teaspoon of chilli powder and a few drops of Tabasco sauce to the mix. Stir thoroughly. Put guacamole in refridgerator to chill until needed.

6. Next for the salsa. Chop the plum tomatoes in a bowl. Add chilli powder, coriander leaves, lime juice and oil. Stir thoroughly. Season with black pepper. Set aside in the refridgerator until needed.

7. Finally, make the tortillas. Sift the flour into a bowl. Gradually add water. Mix together. When you have mixed in half the water, add the oil and mix in. Now gradually add remainder of water (you might need a bit more or a bit less so don't add too much at once) and continue to mix together until you have a smooth dough which leaves the bowl clean.

8. Turn the dough out onto a floured surface. Divide into 8 pieces and roll out each into a thin tortilla.

9. Heat a dry frying pan over a high heat. Cook each tortilla in turn for a few seconds on both sides, flipping the tortilla half way through. Set aside in warm oven until ready to serve.

10. Now add a tablespoon of oil to the frying pan and stir fry the marinaded, chopped Quorn fillet, onion and peppers for 5 minutes.

11. Serve the stir fry with the guacamole, the salsa, grated cheese and soured cream to make up delicious wraps with the warm tortillas.

Calories: 755 kcal per portion (2 wraps with guacamole, salsa, soured cream and cheese)

Moroccan Spicy Tagine with Flatbread

Combining tangy lemon flavor with juicy olives and spices this filling dish is perfect for a Summer evening with friends.

INGREDIENTS (serves 4)

For the tagine:
Quorn fillets (8)
Couscous (300g)
Onion (large)
Green Olives (150g)
Garlic (4 cloves)
Cumin (1 tspn)
Ground Coriander (1 tspn)
Coriander leaves (1 tbspn)
Bird's eye chillis (2)
Lemon juice (20ml)
Chicken (or vegetable) stock cube
Water (500ml)
Sunflower oil (1 tbspn)

For the flatbread:
Strong wholewheat flour (200g)
Salt (1 tspn)
Water (125 ml)

You will need a large mixing bowl, a measuring jug, a large saucepan, a frying pan and 4 individual or 1 family sized tagine(s). If you don't have the tagine(s) then a large casserole dish with lid will work just as well.

Time required: 50 minutes

1. Pre-heat oven to 180 degrees Celsius.

2. Mix the flour and salt in a large bowl. Gradually add cold water, mixing all the time, until the dough sticks together and the sides of the bowl are clean. Turn the dough out onto a work-surface and knead for 5 minutes, flouring the surface as necessary to prevent it sticking. Return kneaded dough to bowl and set aside.

3. Heat the sunflower oil in the frying pan over a medium heat and brown the Quorn fillets for approximately 3 minutes. Remove fillets from pan and turn up heat. Roughly chop onions and add to pan. Fry until starting to blacken at edges (about 4 minutes) then add crushed garlic cloves and turn off heat. Allow to continue cooking for further 2 minutes, stirring continuously.

4. Boil 500ml water and stir in stock cube in measuring jug. Place couscous in large saucepan and add 350ml of the hot stock. Heat over medium heat, stirring with fork. Add cumin, ground coriander and lemon juice. When stock is dissolved into couscous remove from heat.

5. Add fried onions and garlic to spicy couscous. Finely chop bird's eye chillis and add to couscous mix. Add olives to couscous mix.

6. Divide couscous mix into four individual tagines. Divide remaining stock between tagines. Place 2 Quorn fillets on top of couscous mix. Scatter chopped coriander leaves over each tagine. Place tagines in centre of pre-heated oven for 20 minutes.

7. Ten minutes before tagines are due to be removed, divide dough into 8 equal portions. On a floured surface, roll out each portion of dough into a flat circle as thin as you can make it.

8. Heat a clean frying pan over a high heat. When hot, cook flatbreads one at a time, turning them over with a spatula after 30 seconds.

9. Remove tagines from oven and serve immediately with hot flatbreads. For a theatrical flourish, remove the tagine lids at the table (use oven gloves to protect your hands – the lids will be very hot!).

Calories: Tagine 524 kcal per portion, Flatbreads 86 kcal each

Bitterballen

Best for sharing, this Dutch snack is usually served with mustard and a beer.

INGREDIENTS (makes 24 balls which serves 4)

Quorn mince (300g)
Onion (1 small)
Carrot (1 small)
Nutmeg
Parsley (2 tspn)
Lemon juice (20ml)
Black pepper
Margerine (50g)
Plain flour (75g)
Milk (225ml)
Eggs (2 medium)
Breadcrumbs (150g)
Sunflower oil (1 tbspn plus sufficient deep-frying in pan)
Dijon mustard (to serve)

You will need a large mixing bowl, a large saucepan and a deep-frying pan.

Time required: 1 hour 30 minutes

1. Heat the oil in the frying pan over a medium heat. Fry the Quorn mince for 3 minutes, stirring regularly. Finely chop the onion and add this to the pan. Fry for 2 minutes, stirring regularly to mix with the Quorn mince. Peel and grate the carrot. Add this to the pan and fry for 1 minute, stirring constantly to mix with the Quorn mince and onion.

2. Grate a little nutmeg into the mix. Add parsley and lemon juice. Season with black pepper. Cook for 2 minutes. Transfer the mix into a mixing bowl and allow to cool.

3. In a saucepan, melt the margerine over a medium-low heat. Add the flour and stir to make a thick paste. Gradually add the milk, stirring constantly, until you have a thick sauce. Remove from the heat and allow to cool.

4. Combine the Quorn mince mix with the sauce mix in the mixing bowl and stir thoroughly. Place in refridgerator for 45 minutes to 1 hour.

5. Beat eggs in bowl. Prepare breadcrumbs on a large plate.

6. Make the balls by taking about a small golfball sized piece of the combined refridgerated mixture and rolling it between the palms of your hands. You should be able to make about 24 balls with the quantity of mix you've made.

7. Heat approximately 3cm of oil in the deep frying pan. It is ready for cooking when a breadcrumb dropped in the oil sizzles. Be careful not to let the oil get too hot – never leave it unattended.

8. Dip the balls in the beaten eggs, ensuring they are covered, then roll them in the breadcrumbs, making sure that they are coated with crumbs all over.

9. Carefully place the balls in the hot oil so that they don't touch each other. Deep-fry for approximately 1 minute. Remove from the oil and drain excess oil on kitchen roll.

10. Serve the Bitterballen with mustard for dipping.

Calories: 743 kcal per portion of 6 Bitterballen

Quorn Stroganoff

A filling dish that is just what you need on those long, dark Winter nights when the temperature outside has dropped below zero and you feel like you're in Siberia.

INGREDIENTS (serves 4)

Quorn Steak Strips (300g)
Onion (2 large)
Dry white wine (300ml)
Mushrooms (400g)
Soured cream (300ml)
Sunflower oil (1 tbspn)
Beef stock cube
Black pepper
Nutmeg
Long grain rice (300g)

You will need two large saucepans.

Time required: 55 minutes

1. Heat oil over medium heat and soften onions. Add Quorn Steak Strips and fry gently for 2 minutes, stirring continuously.

2. Add wine and stock cube. Turn up heat to high and bring to boil, stirring continuously. Turn heat down to low, cover pan and allow to simmer for 20 minutes, stirring occasionally.

3. Slice mushrooms and add to saucepan. Replace lid and allow to simmer for further 20 minutes, stirring occasionally.

4. While Stroganoff is cooking, bring large pan of water to the boil. Add rice. Stir once and return to boil then cover with lid (offset to prevent boiling over). Cook for 10 minutes.

5. Drain cooked rice in sieve and spoon onto plates to form rings.

6. Pour soured cream onto Stroganoff mix. Add a little grated nutmeg. Stir cream into mix and allow to heat through (1 minute). Spoon Stroganoff mix into centre of rice rings and serve.

Calories: 785 kcal per portion

Haggis wi' 'tatties an' 'neeps

Scotland's "Great chieftain o' the pudding-race". Many years ago, this was my first venture into vegetarian cooking, one Burns Night, for my then girlfriend, who was vegetarian some years before I became one. Suffice to say that my attempt was a disaster, which she described as "chillied porridge". Hopefully my cooking has improved somewhat since then and the fault must be attributed to "user error" rather than anything to do with the excellent recipe.

INGREDIENTS (serves 4)

Quorn Mince (300g)
Onion (3 large)
Oatmeal (225g)
Ground coriander (1 tspn)
Mace (1 tspn)
Nutmeg
Beef stock cubes (2)
Black pepper
Sunflower oil (1 tbspn)
Potatoes (800g)
Turnips (400g)
Margerine (50g)

Double cream (4 tbspn)
Plain flour (1 tspn)
Whisky (1 dram of Scotch i.e. 3½ml)

You will need two large saucepans, one with lid, a mixing bowl and a potato masher.

Time required: 50 minutes

1. Preheat oven to 200 degrees Celsius.

2. Finely chop two of the onions. Mix in bowl with the oatmeal. Add coriander, mace and a half a grated nutmeg. Season with black pepper and mix thoroughly.

3. Dissolve a beef stock cube in 500ml of boiled water. Add stock a little at a time, stirring each time, until the mixture starts to bind. Now add the Quorn mince and stir in. Continue to add the stock a little at a time to the haggis mix and stir until it has a moist, sticky consistency.

4. Spoon the mix into a casserole and place in the centre of the pre-heated oven to bake for 40 minutes. I like to use individual casseroles to serve at the table – in which case you may need to reduce the cooking time a little.

5. When there are 25 minutes cooking time left for the haggis, peel the potatoes and turnip. Chop them into small pieces. Bring a large saucepan of water to the boil. Add the potatoes and turnips. When the water has returned to the boil, turn down the heat, cover and leave to simmer for 20 minutes.

6. Drain the potatoes and turnips. You can add the water to any stock you have left from making the haggis ready to use to make the gravy. Separate the potatoes from the turnips.

7. Mash the potatoes with half the margerine and double cream. Mash the turnips with the other half of the margerine and double cream.

8. In a clean pan, heat the sunflower oil over a medium heat. Chop the third onion and soften in the oil for 3 minutes. Add the beef stock and dissolve the second beef stock cube in the gravy. Make up a paste with the plain flour and a little cold water. Stir into the gravy. Finally, add the

whisky to the gravy.

9. Serve the haggis, mashed potatoes and mashed turnips drizzled with the gravy.

Calories: 820 kcal per portion

Singapore Stir Fried Noodles

A staple dish of south east Asia which comes in many varieties. Try it with prawns for a delicious variation on the recipe here.

INGREDIENTS (serves 4)

Quorn Chicken Pieces (200g)
Quorn Bacon Slices (4 rashers)
Shiitake Mushrooms (100g)
Ginger (5cm root, grated or 1 tspn powder)
Red chilli (2)
Turmeric (2 tspn)
Red pepper (1)
Carrot (2 medium)
Bean sprouts (100g)
Bird's eye chilli (2)
Soy sauce (2 tspn)
Oyster sauce (2 tspn)
Rice vinegar (2 tspn)
Egg (1)
Sunflower oil (1 tbspn)

Vermicelli rice noodles (300g)
Spring onions (4)

You will need a large wok or frying pan and a sieve.

Time required: 15 minutes

1. Cut the chillis horizontally into rings approximately ½ cm wide. Deseed. Heat oil over medium heat and fry the ginger, chillis, mushrooms and turmeric for 30 seconds, stirring constantly.

2. Slice red pepper lengthways and deseed. Peel carrots and cut lengthways into thin strips. Add pepper, bean sprouts, carrots and Quorn Chicken Pieces. Cook for 2 minutes, stirring constantly.

3. Soak noodles for 1 minute in boiled water. Drain and add to stir fry. Cook for 2 minutes.

4. Chop the bird's eye chillis. Add chillis to stir fry. Add Soy sauce, Oyster sauce and rice vinegar. Stir to ensure all are thoroughly mixed into the stir fry. Cook for 1 minute.

5. Cut Quorn bacon slices lengthways into thin strips. Add Quorn bacon slices to stir fry. Cook for 1 minute.

6. Beat egg. Add beaten egg to stir fry. Mix thoroughly with noodles. Cook for 2 minutes.

7. Serve on plates, garnished with chopped spring onions.

Calories: 470 kcal per portion

Basque Quorn

A spicy dish from the northern part of Spain that blends the tastes of olives, red wine and paprika.

INGREDIENTS (serves 4)

Quorn Chicken Pieces (300g)
Quorn Chorizo slices (100g)
Green pepper (2)
Onion (2 medium)
Garlic (1 clove)
Tomatoes (400g)
Green olives (100g)
Chicken stock cube
Red wine (175ml)
Tomato purée double concentrate (1 tbspn)
Paprika (1 tspn)
Basil (1 tspn)
Black pepper
Long grain rice (300g)
Sunflower oil (1 tbspn)

You will need a large saucepan with a lid.

Time required: 40 minutes

1. Heat the oil in the pan over a medium heat. Brown the Quorn Chicken Pieces for 2 minutes, stirring regularly.

2. De-seed and chop the green pepper. Roughly chop the onion. Finely chop the garlic. Add to the pan and cook for 3 minutes, stirring regularly.

3. Roughly chop the tomatoes and add to the pan. Cook for 2 minutes. Stirring constantly.

4. Add the rice. Stir to ensure the rice is well covered and mixed in. Cook for 2 minutes.

5. Dissolve the chicken stock cube in 250ml of boiled water. Add the stock, red wine, tomato purée, basil and paprika. Season with black pepper. Stir to ensure all are thoroughly mixed together. Bring to the simmering point. Reduce heat, cover and cook for 20 minutes. Stir occasionally and top up with hot water if it becomes too dry and rice begins to stick to bottom of the pan.

6. Add the Quorn Chorizo slices and olives. Cook uncovered for 10 minutes, stirring regularly.

7. Serve immediately.

Calories: 622 kcal per portion

Paella

Not strictly speaking vegetarian but it is such a fabulous, traditional Spanish dish that I just had to include it.

INGREDIENTS (serves 4)

Quorn Fillets (8)
Quorn Chorizo (16 slices)
King Prawns (200g, raw)
Mussels (200g)
Onion (2 large, roughly chopped)
Sunflower oil (2-3 tbspn)
Chicken stock cube
Saffron (2 pinches)
Garlic (2 cloves, finely chopped)
Paprika (1 tsp)
Black pepper
Peas (200g)
Red/Green/Yellow Pepper (2 – mix'n'match colours to suit you!)
Spanish Paella rice (300g)
Parsley (1 tsp)

You will need a large, deep frying pan with a lid (a wok is perfect) and a small bowl.

Time required: 35 minutes

1. Place saffron in small bowl containing 100ml of hot water.

2. Heat oil over medium heat and brown the Quorn fillets, turning frequently. Add Chorizo slices and continue to turn frequently for 1 minute.

3. Turn heat down a little and add chopped onions. Soften onions for 2 minutes, stirring continuously (and keep turning the fillets and chorizo).

4. Add chopped garlic and paprika. Continue to stir over low heat for further 2 minutes.

5. Add rice and peas. Stir thoroughly. Dissolve chicken stock cube in 1.25 litres of hot water and pour into paella mix. Add saffron flavoured water. Season with black pepper. Stir again and turn up heat to bring back to boil.

6. Lower heat and allow to simmer for 12 minutes.

7. Add prawns, mussels and chopped peppers on top of paella mix. Top up with a little more water if all liquid absorbed already. Put lid on frying pan. Leave to cook for 5 minutes – until prawns turn pink.

8. Serve immediately. Top off with chopped parsley.

Calories: 733 kcal per portion

Rösti mit Spiegel Ei

The Alpine Swiss answer to the All Day Breakfast question. Filling and satisfying with different fillings, such as cheese and onions, depending on the Canton. This recipe sticks to the simple inclusion of bacon and a fried egg topping.

INGREDIENTS (per person)

Quorn Bacon Slices (2)
Potatoes (100g)
Egg (1 medium)
Black pepper
Sunflower oil (1 tbspn)

You will need a large frying pan and a mixing bowl..

Time required: 15 minutes

1. Grate potatoes into a tea towel or muslin. Squeeze out excess moisture. Place in mixing bowl. Roughly chop the Quorn Bacon Slices. Add to

the bowl and stir to mix in thoroughly. Season with black pepper.

2. Heat oil in frying pan over medium high heat. Add potato mix to pan and press into firm round about 2 cm thick. Fry for 4 minutes.

3. Using a spatula, carefully flip the fried rösti cake. Fry on other side for 4 minutes. Turn out onto plate.

4. Fry egg, sunny side up, in pan. You can cook the yolk by tipping the pan slightly so that a pool of hot oil collects that can be spooned over the yolk. Add fried to top of rösti cake to serve.

Calories: 385 kcal per portion

Green Curry with Sticky Rice

For the authentic taste of this exquisitely spiced dish you need to make up the curry paste immediately before cooking as they do in Thailand.

INGREDIENTS (serves 4)

Quorn Chicken Pieces (300g)
Green chilli (2)
Onions (2 medium)
Ginger (2.5cm root, grated or ½ tspn powder)
Coriander leaves (2 tspn)
Lemon Grass (4 tspn)
Lime Juice (3 tspn)
Kaffir Lime leaves (6)
Galangal (2 tspn)
Ground Coriander (2 tspn)
Cumin (1 tspn)
Thai Fish Sauce (2 tspn)
Black pepper
Sunflower oil (2 tbspn)
Sugar (1 tbspn, brown)
Coconut milk (400ml)
Thai Sticky Rice (300g)

You will need a large wok or frying pan, a steamer pan and a mixing bowl..

Time required: 30 minutes plus overnight soak for sticky rice

1. Place sticky rice in large bowl of cold water overnight. Drain. Line the steamer with muslin and place rice in steamer. Bring water to boil in lower pan and steam for 25 to 30 minutes.

2. De-seed and finely chop the green chillis and place in bowl. Finely chop onions and add to bowl. Grate the ginger and add to bowl. Finely chop the kaffir lime leaves and add to bowl. Add coriander leaves, lime juice, chopped lemon grass stalk, galangal paste, ground coriander and cumin. Stir vigourously to mix the ingredients thoroughly then season with black pepper. Add thai fish sauce and 1 tablespoon of sunflower oil. Stir until incorporated into a thick paste.

3. Heat tablespoon of sunflower oil in wok over a high heat. Add the green curry paste and sugar. Cook for 1 minute, stirring continuously.

4. Reduce heat and add Quorn chicken pieces. Cook for 3 minutes, stirring continuously.

5. Add coconut milk. Return to simmer and then turn heat down. Leave to simmer for 20 minutes, stirring occasionally.

6. When steamed rice is cooked, transfer to bowls and spoon the green curry over the top.

Calories: 707 kcal per portion

Pad Thai

In Thailand they ask you how hot you want this dish. I've eaten mild versions which had only minimal kick through to searingly hot recipes that left my tastebuds zinging for hours afterwards. You can also vary the heat by increasing or decreasing the amount of chilli and ginger you use.

INGREDIENTS (serves 4)

Quorn Chicken Pieces (300g)
Onions (2 medium, roughly chopped)
Bird's eye chillis (3)
Garlic (2 cloves, finely chopped)
Ginger (2.5cm root, grated or ½ tspn powder)
Bean sprouts (100g)
Coriander leaves (3 tspn)
Lime Juice (4 tspn)
Thai Fish Sauce (4 tspn)
Black pepper
Eggs (2)
Sunflower oil (2 tbspn)
Rice noodles (300g)
Roasted salted peanuts (4 tspns)

You will need a large wok or frying pan, a large pan and a sieve.

Time required: 20 minutes

1. Heat the oil over a high heat in the wok and brown the Quorn Chicken pieces for 2 minutes, stirring constantly. Remove and set aside.

2. Add the chopped onion to the wok together with chopped chillis, garlic and ginger. And fry for 1 minute, stirring constantly.

3. Add the chicken and bean sprouts to the wok and fry for further 2 minutes, stirring occasionally.

4. Place the rice noodles in pan of boiling water and cook for 1 minute, teasing the bundles apart with a fork.

5. Drain the noodles in a sieve and add to the wok. Stir thoroughly. Add the fish sauce and lime juice. Season with black pepper. Stir again to ensure all ingredients are thoroughly mixed. Cook for 2 minutes.

6. Beat eggs and stir into mix, ensuring noodles are well coated. Add half the coriander leaves. Crush the roasted salted peanuts and add half to the mix. Cook for 2 minutes.

7. Serve in bowls. Garnish with remainder of coriander leaves and crushed peanuts.

Calories: 550 kcal per portion

Red Curry with Jasmine Rice

A strongly flavoured curry from Thailand, traditionally served with Jasmine Rice.

INGREDIENTS (serves 4)

Quorn Steak Strips (300g)
Bird's eye chilli (4)
Ginger (5cm root, grated or 1 tspn powder)
Lemon Grass (4 tspn)
Onion (2 medium)
Garlic (4 cloves)
Ground Coriander (2 tspn)
Cumin (1 tspn)
Thai Fish Sauce (2 tspn)
Black pepper
Sunflower oil (2 tbspn)
Tamarind paste (1 tspn)
Coconut milk (400ml)
Thai Jasmine Rice (200g)

You will need a large wok or frying pan, a large saucepan, a sieve and a mixing bowl..

Time required: 30 minutes

1. Meanwhile finely chop the bird's eye chillis, onions and garlic and place in bowl. Grate the ginger and add to bowl. Stir thoroughly. Add chopped lemon grass stalk, ground coriander and cumin. Stir vigourously to mix the ingredients thoroughly then season with black pepper. Add a little water and stir until incorporated into a thick paste.

2. Bring large pan of water to the boil. Add jasmine rice. Stir once and return to boil then cover with lid (offset to prevent boiling over). Cook for 15 minutes.

3. Heat tablespoon of sunflower oil in wok over a high heat. Add the red curry paste and cook for 1 minute, stirring continuously.

4. Reduce heat and add Quorn Steak Strips. Cook for 3 minutes, stirring continuously.

5. Add tamarind paste and Thai fish sauce then cook for 2 minutes, stirring continuously.

6. Add coconut milk and stir in. Bring to simmer and then turn heat down. Leave to simmer for 15 minutes, stirring occasionally.

7. Drain cooked jasmine rice in sieve. Lightly oil a small bowl and press quarter of rice into bowl. Quickly invert onto plate and remove bowl. Repeat onto separate plates for each serving.

8. Spoon the red curry onto the plate beside the rice.

Calories: 600 kcal per portion

Stuffed Peppers

With the exotic smell of cinnamon filling the kitchen as it cooks, this Turkish dish is a great favourite of mine.

INGREDIENTS (serves 4)

Quorn Mince (400g)
Onion (2 large, roughly chopped)
Sunflower oil (2 tbspn)
Beef stock cube
Garlic (2 cloves, finely chopped)
Italian plum tomatoes (400g tin)
Cinnamon (1 tspn)
Oregano (1 tspn)
Black pepper
Red and Green Peppers (4 of each)
Long grain rice (300g)

You will need two large saucepans, a baking tray and a sieve.

Time required: 55 minutes

1. Pre-heat the oven to 200 degrees Celsius.

2. Heat 1 tablespoon of oil in a pan over a medium heat. Add rice and stir to coat the rice. Boil water in kettle and pour over rice so that the rie is covered with plenty of water to spare. Return to boil then turn down heat, cover with lid and leave to cook for 10 minutes.

3. In second pan, heat remaining oil over medium heat and gently fry onion and garlic for 3 minutes. Add the Quorn mince. Crumble the beef stock into the pan and add the cinnamon and oregano. Season with black pepper. Cook for 2 minutes.

4. Reduce heat. Add the tomatoes and chop them roughly with a knife while they cook. Cook for 5 minutes, stirring regularly.

5. Drain the rice in the sieve and add it to the other pan. Stir thoroughly to coat the rice with the juices.

6. Cut the top off the peppers and de-seed them. Place on baking tray, propped upright against each other. Spoon the mix into the peppers, packing it down.

7. Place baking tray on middle shelf of pre-heated oven and cook the stuffed peppers for 30 minutes.

8. Serve immediately with cooked lids on the peppers or beside them, as takes your fancy.

Calories: 582 kcal per portion

Vietnamese Noodle Soup

Don't be fooled by the name, this soup is a whole meal in itself.

INGREDIENTS (serves 4)

Quorn Steak Strips (300g)
Onion (2 medium, roughly chopped)
Garlic (2 cloves, finely chopped)
Green chilli (2)
Beef stock cube
Black pepper
Egg noodles (250g)
Coriander leaves (2 tspn)
Sunflower oil (1 tbspn)

You will need two large saucepans and a sieve.

Time required: 20 minutes

1. Heat the oil in a large pan over a high heat and brown the Quorn Steak

Strips for 2 minutes, stirring constantly. Season with black pepper.

2. Cut the chillis horizontally into rings approximately ½ cm wide. Deseed. Add chillis, roughly chopped onion and finely chopped garlic to the pan. Lower heat and cook for 3 minutes, stirring occasionally.

3. Dissolve beef stock cube in 500ml of boiled water. Add to pan, stir and bring to simmering point. Simmer for 10 minutes.

4. Meanwhile, bring second pan of water to boil. Add egg noodles. Cook for 4 minutes.

5. Drain noodles and add to soup. Cook for further 3 minutes.

6. Spoon the noodles and soup into bowls and garnish with coriander leaves.

Calories: 296 kcal per portion

Index

American (Hot) Pepperoni Pizza
Arborio rice
- Italian Casserole with Risotto alla Milanese
- Quorn Risotto

Aubergine
- Moussaka

Avocado
- Chilli con Quorn with Guacamole
- Quorn Fajitas

Baby vine tomatoes
- Quorn Risotto

Baked Beans
- Full English Breakfast

Balsamic vinegar
- Quorn Risotto

Bamboo shoots
- Quorn and Cashew Nuts with Rice
- Sweet and Sour Quorn

Basil
- Basque Quorn
- Lasagna al Forno
- Spaghetti Bolognese

Basmati Rice
- Quorn Biryani
- Quorn Korma with Pilau Rice and Naan Bread
- Quorn Tikka Masala with Rice and Naan Bread
- Tandoori Quorn with Saffron Rice

Bay leaf
- Bangers and Mash with red wine gravy
- Carbonnade à la Flamande avec Frites
- Lancashire Hotpot
- Quorn Bourguignonne with Dauphinois Potatoes
- Quorn Korma with Pilau Rice and Naan Bread
- Quorn au Pot with Boulangère Potatoes
- Quorn au Vin with Lyonnaise Potatoes
- Quorn Vindaloo

Bean sprouts
- Pad Thai
- Quorn Chow Mein

- Singapore Stir Fried Noodles

Beef stock cube
- Carbonnade à la Flamande avec Frites
- Chilli con Quorn with Guacamole
- Cornish Pasty
- Cottage Pie
- Haggis wi' 'tatties an' 'neeps
- Hungarian Goulash
- Irish Stew and Dumplings
- Lancashire Hotpot
- Lasagna al Forno
- Moussaka
- Quorn in Ale Pudding
- Quorn Madras with Bombay Potatoes
- Quorn Stroganoff
- Spaghetti Bolognese
- Stuffed Peppers
- Toad in the Hole
- Vietnamese Noodle Soup

Belgian Beer
- Carbonnade à la Flamande avec Frites

Bicarbonate of soda
- Quorn Korma with Pilau Rice and Naan Bread
- Quorn Tikka Masala with Rice and Naan Bread

Bird's eye chillis
- American (Hot) Pepperoni Pizza
- Mole Quorn
- Moroccan Spicy Tagine with Flatbread
- Pad Thai
- Red Curry with Jasmine Rice
- Singapore Stir Fried Noodles

Black pepper
- American (Hot) Pepperoni Pizza
- Bangers and Mash with red wine gravy
- Basque Quorn
- Bitterballen
- Carbonnade à la Flamande avec Frites
- Chilli con Quorn with Guacamole
- Cornish Pasty
- Cottage Pie
- Green Curry with Sticky Rice
- Haggis wi' 'tatties an' 'neeps
- Hungarian Goulash

- Irish Stew and Dumplings
- Italian Casserole with Risotto alla Milanese
- Lancashire Hotpot
- Lasagna al Forno
- Moussaka
- Pad Thai
- Paella
- Paprika Quorn Fillets
- Quorn in Ale Pudding
- Quorn Bourguignonne with Dauphinois Potatoes
- Quorn Fajitas
- Quorn Korma with Pilau Rice and Naan Bread
- Quorn au Pot with Boulangère Potatoes
- Quorn Risotto
- Quorn Stroganoff
- Quorn au Vin with Lyonnaise Potatoes
- Red Curry with Jasmine Rice
- Rösti mit Spiegel Ei
- Southern Fried Quorn Fillets
- Spaghetti Bolognese
- Stuffed Peppers
- Tagliatelle Carbonara
- Tartiflette
- Toad in the Hole
- Traditional Sunday Roast with Yorkshire Pudding
- Vietnamese Noodle Soup

Bread
- Bitterballen
- Full English Breakfast
- Southern Fried Quorn Fillets
- Traditional Sunday Roast with Yorkshire Pudding

Carbonnade à la Flamande avec Frites
Cardomam Pods
- Quorn Korma with Pilau Rice and Naan Bread

Carrot
- Bitterballen
- Cottage Pie
- Irish Stew and Dumplings
- Quorn in Ale Pudding
- Quorn and Cashew Nuts with Rice
- Quorn Chow Mein
- Quorn au Pot with Boulangère Potatoes

- Singapore Stir Fried Noodles
- Sweet and Sour Quorn
- Traditional Sunday Roast with Yorkshire Pudding

Cashew Nuts
- Quorn and Cashew Nuts with Rice

Cayenne Pepper
- Paprika Quorn Fillets
- Quorn Vindaloo
- Southern Fried Quorn Fillets

Cheddar cheese
- Cottage Pie
- Quorn Fajitas

Chicken stock cube
- Basque Quorn
- Italian Casserole with Risotto alla Milanese
- Moroccan Spicy Tagine with Flatbread
- Paella
- Paprika Quorn Fillets
- Quorn and Cashew Nuts with Rice
- Quorn Korma with Pilau Rice and Naan Bread
- Quorn au Pot with Boulangère Potatoes
- Quorn Risotto
- Quorn Tikka Masala with Rice and Naan Bread
- Quorn au Vin with Lyonnaise Potatoes
- Traditional Sunday Roast with Yorkshire Pudding

Chilli con Quorn with Guacamole

Chilli powder
- Chilli con Quorn with Guacamole
- Quorn Biryani
- Quorn Fajitas
- Quorn Korma with Pilau Rice and Naan Bread
- Quorn Madras with Bombay Potatoes
- Quorn Tikka Masala with Rice and Naan Bread
- Quorn Vindaloo
- Tandoori Quorn with Saffron Rice

Chocolate (dark)
- Mole Quorn

Cinnamon
- Cottage Pie
- Mole Quorn
- Moussaka
- Quorn Biryani
- Quorn Vindaloo

Cloves
- Quorn Korma with Pilau Rice and Naan Bread

Coconut milk
- Green Curry with Sticky Rice
- Red Curry with Jasmine Rice

Coriander (Ground)
- Green Curry with Sticky Rice
- Haggis wi' 'tatties an' 'neeps
- Moroccan Spicy Tagine with Flatbread
- Quorn Biryani
- Quorn Korma with Pilau Rice and Naan Bread
- Quorn Tikka Masala with Rice and Naan Bread
- Quorn Vindaloo
- Red Curry with Jasmine Rice

Coriander leaves
- Green Curry with Sticky Rice
- Mole Quorn
- Moroccan Spicy Tagine with Flatbread
- Pad Thai
- Quorn Fajitas
- Quorn Korma with Pilau Rice and Naan Bread
- Quorn Madras with Bombay Potatoes
- Quorn Tikka Masala with Rice and Naan Bread
- Vietnamese Noodle Soup

Cornish Pasty

Cottage Pie

Couscous
- Moroccan Spicy Tagine with Flatbread

Cumin
- Green Curry with Sticky Rice
- Mole Quorn
- Moroccan Spicy Tagine with Flatbread
- Quorn Biryani
- Quorn Fajitas
- Quorn Korma with Pilau Rice and Naan Bread
- Quorn Madras with Bombay Potatoes
- Quorn Tikka Masala with Rice and Naan Bread
- Quorn Vindaloo
- Red Curry with Jasmine Rice

Double cream
- Bangers and Mash with red wine gravy

- Cottage Pie
- Haggis wi' 'tatties an' 'neeps
- Lasagna al Forno
- Quorn Bourguignonne with Dauphinois Potatoes
- Quorn Korma with Pilau Rice and Naan Bread
- Quorn Tikka Masala with Rice and Naan Bread
- Tartiflette

Egg
- Bitterballen
- Cornish Pasty
- Full English Breakfast
- Moussaka
- Pad Thai
- Quorn Fried Rice
- Quorn Korma with Pilau Rice and Naan Bread
- Quorn Tikka Masala with Rice and Naan Bread
- Rösti mit Spiegel Ei
- Singapore Stir Fried Noodles
- Southern Fried Quorn Fillets
- Tagliatelle Carbonara
- Toad in the Hole
- Traditional Sunday Roast with Yorkshire Pudding

English Ale
- Quorn in Ale Pudding

Fennel seeds
- Quorn Korma with Pilau Rice and Naan Bread
- Quorn Tikka Masala with Rice and Naan Bread

Flour (plain)
- Bitterballen
- Cornish Pasty
- Haggis wi' 'tatties an' 'neeps
- Lasagna al Forno
- Moussaka
- Paprika Quorn Fillets
- Quorn and Cashew Nuts with Rice
- Quorn Fajitas
- Quorn Korma with Pilau Rice and Naan Bread
- Quorn au Pot with Boulangère Potatoes
- Quorn au Vin with Lyonnaise Potatoes
- Toad in the Hole
- Traditional Sunday Roast with Yorkshire Pudding

Flour (self-raising)
- Irish Stew and Dumplings
- Quorn in Ale Pudding

Flour (strong, white)
- American (Hot) Pepperoni Pizza
- Quorn Korma with Pilau Rice and Naan Bread
- Quorn Tikka Masala with Rice and Naan Bread

Flour (strong, wholewheat)
- Moroccan Spicy Tagine with Flatbread

French bread
- Carbonnade à la Flamande avec Frites

Full English Breakfast

Galangal
- Green Curry with Sticky Rice

Garam Masala
- Quorn Madras with Bombay Potatoes
- Tandoori Quorn with Saffron Rice

Garlic
- American (Hot) Pepperoni Pizza
- Bangers and Mash with red wine gravy
- Basque Quorn
- Carbonnade à la Flamande avec Frites
- Chilli con Quorn with Guacamole
- Hungarian Goulash
- Italian Casserole with Risotto alla Milanese
- Lasagna al Forno
- Mole Quorn
- Moroccan Spicy Tagine with Flatbread
- Moussaka
- Pad Thai
- Paella
- Quorn Biryani
- Quorn Bourguignonne with Dauphinois Potatoes
- Quorn Fajitas
- Quorn Korma with Pilau Rice and Naan Bread
- Quorn Madras with Bombay Potatoes
- Quorn au Pot with Boulangère Potatoes
- Quorn Risotto
- Quorn Tikka Masala with Rice and Naan Bread
- Quorn au Vin with Lyonnaise Potatoes
- Quorn Vindaloo
- Red Curry with Jasmine Rice

- Spaghetti Bolognese
- Stuffed Peppers
- Tagliatelle Carbonara
- Tandoori Quorn with Saffron Rice
- Tartiflette
- Vietnamese Noodle Soup

Ginger
- Green Curry with Sticky Rice
- Pad Thai
- Quorn Biryani
- Quorn Korma with Pilau Rice and Naan Bread
- Quorn Madras with Bombay Potatoes
- Quorn Tikka Masala with Rice and Naan Bread
- Quorn Vindaloo
- Red Curry with Jasmine Rice
- Singapore Stir Fried Noodles
- Tandoori Quorn with Saffron Rice

Green chilli
- Green Curry with Sticky Rice
- Vietnamese Noodle Soup

Green Curry with Sticky Rice

Green pepper
- American (Hot) Pepperoni Pizza
- Basque Quorn
- Paella
- Paprika Quorn Fillets
- Quorn and Cashew Nuts with Rice
- Quorn Fajitas
- Stuffed Peppers

Gruyère cheese
- Carbonnade à la Flamande avec Frites
- Moussaka

Honey
- Traditional Sunday Roast with Yorkshire Pudding

Hungarian Goulash

Irish Stew and Dumplings
Italian Casserole with Risotto alla Milanese

Kaffir lime leaves
- Green Curry with Sticky Rice

King prawns

- Paella

Lasagna
- Lasagna al Forno
Lancashire Hotpot
Lasagna al Forno
Lemon Grass
- Green Curry with Sticky Rice
- Red Curry with Jasmine Rice
Lemon juice
- Bitterballen
- Chilli con Quorn with Guacamole
- Moroccan Spicy Tagine with Flatbread
- Quorn Fajitas
Lime juice
- Green Curry with Sticky Rice
- Pad Thai
- Quorn Fajitas
- Quorn Tikka Masala with Rice and Naan Bread
- Tandoori Quorn with Saffron Rice

Mace
- Haggis wi' 'tatties an' 'neeps
Margerine
- Bangers and Mash with red wine gravy
- Bitterballen
- Cornish Pasty
- Cottage Pie
- Haggis wi' 'tatties an' 'neeps
- Lancashire Hotpot
- Lasagna al Forno
- Moussaka
- Quorn in Ale Pudding
- Quorn Bourguignonne with Dauphinois Potatoes
- Quorn au Vin with Lyonnaise Potatoes
Milk
- Bitterballen
- Lasagna al Forno
- Moussaka
- Quorn Bourguignonne with Dauphinois Potatoes
- Quorn Korma with Pilau Rice and Naan Bread
- Quorn au Pot with Boulangère Potatoes
- Quorn Tikka Masala with Rice and Naan Bread

- Toad in the Hole
- Traditional Sunday Roast with Yorkshire Pudding

Mole Quorn
Moroccan Spicy Tagine with Flatbread
Moussaka

Mozzarella cheese
- American (Hot) Pepperoni Pizza

Mushrooms
- Bangers and Mash with red wine gravy
- Full English Breakfast
- Quorn Bourguignonne with Dauphinois Potatoes
- Quorn Stroganoff
- Quorn au Vin with Lyonnaise Potatoes

Mussels
- Paella

Mustard (Dijon)
- Bitterballen

Mustard powder
- Carbonnade à la Flamande avec Frites
- Quorn Madras with Bombay Potatoes
- Quorn Vindaloo

Noodles (egg)
- Quorn Chow Mein
- Vietnamese Noodle Soup

Nutmeg
- Bitterballen
- Haggis wi' 'tatties an' 'neeps
- Lasagna al Forno
- Moussaka
- Quorn Biryani
- Quorn Bourguignonne with Dauphinois Potatoes
- Quorn Stroganoff

Oatmeal
- Haggis wi' 'tatties an' 'neeps

Olives (Green)
- Basque Quorn
- Moroccan Spicy Tagine with Flatbread

Olive oil
- American (Hot) Pepperoni Pizza
- Carbonnade à la Flamande avec Frites
- Quorn Korma with Pilau Rice and Naan Bread

Cooking with Quorn: 50 Meals From Around The World

- Quorn Risotto
- Quorn Tikka Masala with Rice and Naan Bread

Onion
- American (Hot) Pepperoni Pizza
- Bangers and Mash with red wine gravy
- Bitterballen
- Carbonnade à la Flamande avec Frites
- Chilli con Quorn with Guacamole
- Cornish Pasty
- Cottage Pie
- Green Curry with Sticky Rice
- Haggis wi' 'tatties an' 'neeps
- Hungarian Goulash
- Irish Stew and Dumplings
- Italian Casserole with Risotto alla Milanese
- Lancashire Hotpot
- Lasagna al Forno
- Mole Quorn
- Moroccan Spicy Tagine with Flatbread
- Moussaka
- Pad Thai
- Paella
- Paprika Quorn Fillets
- Quorn in Ale Pudding
- Quorn Biryani
- Quorn Bourguignonne with Dauphinois Potatoes
- Quorn and Cashew Nuts with Rice
- Quorn Fajitas
- Quorn Korma with Pilau Rice and Naan Bread
- Quorn Madras with Bombay Potatoes
- Quorn au Pot with Boulangère Potatoes
- Quorn Risotto
- Quorn Stroganoff
- Quorn Tikka Masala with Rice and Naan Bread
- Quorn au Vin with Lyonnaise Potatoes
- Quorn Vindaloo
- Red Curry with Jasmine Rice
- Spaghetti Bolognese
- Stuffed Peppers
- Sweet and Sour Quorn
- Tandoori Quorn with Saffron Rice
- Tartiflette
- Toad in the Hole

- Traditional Sunday Roast with Yorkshire Pudding
- Vietnamese Noodle Soup

Orange juice
- Sweet and Sour Quorn

Oregano
- American (Hot) Pepperoni Pizza
- Quorn Risotto
- Southern Fried Quorn Fillets
- Stuffed Peppers

Oyster sauce
- Singapore Stir Fried Noodles

Pad Thai
Paella
Paprika
- Basque Quorn
- Hungarian Goulash
- Paella
- Paprika Quorn Fillets
- Quorn Fajitas
- Quorn Vindaloo

Paprika Quorn Fillets
Parmesan cheese
- Italian Casserole with Risotto alla Milanese
- Lasagna al Forno
- Quorn Risotto
- Spaghetti Bolognese
- Tagliatelle Carbonara

Parsley
- Bitterballen
- Cottage Pie
- Irish Stew and Dumplings
- Italian Casserole with Risotto alla Milanese
- Moussaka
- Paella
- Quorn au Pot with Boulangère Potatoes

Parsnip
- Traditional Sunday Roast with Yorkshire Pudding

Peanut butter
- Mole Quorn

Pearl Barley
- Irish Stew and Dumplings

Peas

- Paella
- Quorn Fried Rice
- Quorn Risotto

Pineapple chunks
- Sweet and Sour Quorn

Plum Tomatoes
- American (Hot) Pepperoni Pizza
- Hungarian Goulash
- Lasagna al Forno
- Mole Quorn
- Moussaka
- Paprika Quorn Fillets
- Quorn Fajitas
- Spaghetti Bolognese
- Stuffed Peppers

Potatoes
- Bangers and Mash with red wine gravy
- Carbonnade à la Flamande avec Frites
- Cornish Pasty
- Cottage Pie
- Haggis wi' 'tatties an' 'neeps
- Irish Stew and Dumplings
- Lancashire Hotpot
- Quorn in Ale Pudding
- Quorn Bourguignonne with Dauphinois Potatoes
- Quorn Madras with Bombay Potatoes
- Quorn au Pot with Boulangère Potatoes
- Quorn au Vin with Lyonnaise Potatoes
- Rösti mit Spiegel Ei
- Southern Fried Quorn Fillets
- Tartiflette
- Traditional Sunday Roast with Yorkshire Pudding

Quorn in Ale Pudding

Quorn bacon rashers
- Full English Breakfast
- Rösti mit Spiegel Ei
- Singapore Stir Fried Noodles
- Tagliatelle Carbonara
- Tartiflette

Quorn Biryani
Quorn Bourguignonne with Dauphinois Potatoes
Quorn and Cashew Nuts with Rice

Quorn chicken pieces
- Basque Quorn
- Green Curry with Sticky Rice
- Pad Thai
- Quorn Biryani
- Quorn and Cashew Nuts with Rice
- Quorn Risotto
- Quorn Korma with Pilau Rice and Naan Bread
- Quorn Tikka Masala with Rice and Naan Bread
- Singapore Stir Fried Noodles
- Sweet and Sour Quorn
- Quorn chorizo slices
  -Basque Quorn

Paella

Quorn Chow Mein

Quorn Fajitas

Quorn Family Roast
- Quorn au Pot with Boulangère Potatoes
- Traditional Sunday Roast with Yorkshire Pudding

Quorn fillets
- Italian Casserole with Risotto alla Milanese
- Mole Quorn
- Moroccan Spicy Tagine with Flatbread
- Paella
- Quorn Fajitas
- Quorn au Vin with Lyonnaise Potatoes
- Paprika Quorn Fillets
- Southern Fried Quorn Fillets
- Tandoori Quorn with Saffron Rice

Quorn Fried Rice

Quorn Madras with Bombay Potatoes

Quorn mince
- Bitterballen
- Chilli con Quorn with Guacamole
- Cornish Pasty
- Cottage Pie
- Haggis wi' 'tatties an' 'neeps
- Lasagna al Forno
- Moussaka
- Spaghetti Bolognese
- Stuffed Peppers

Quorn pepperoni slices
- American (Hot) Pepperoni Pizza

Quorn au Pot with Boulangère Potatoes
Quorn Risotto
Quorn sausage
- Bangers and Mash with red wine gravy
- Full English Breakfast
- Toad in the Hole

Quorn Stroganoff
Quorn steak strips
- Carbonnade à la Flamande avec Frites
- Hungarian Goulash
- Irish Stew and Dumplings
- Lancashire Hotpot
- Quorn in Ale Pudding
- Quorn Bourguignonne with Dauphinois Potatoes
- Quorn Chow Mein
- Quorn Fried Rice
- Quorn Madras with Bombay Potatoes
- Quorn Stroganoff
- Quorn Vindaloo
- Red Curry with Jasmine Rice
- Vietnamese Noodle Soup

Quorn Tikka Masala with Rice and Naan Bread
Quorn au Vin with Lyonnaise Potatoes
Quorn Vindaloo

Reblochon cheese
- Tartiflette

Red chilli
- Singapore Stir Fried Noodles

Red kidney beans
- Hungarian Goulash
- Chilli con Quorn with Guacamole

Red lentil
- Quorn Madras with Bombay Potatoes

Red pepper
- Chilli con Quorn with Guacamole
- Paella
- Quorn Fajitas
- Singapore Stir Fried Noodles
- Stuffed Peppers

Red wine
- Bangers and Mash with red wine gravy
- Basque Quorn

- Lasagna al Forno
- Moussaka
- Quorn Bourguignonne with Dauphinois Potatoes
- Quorn au Vin with Lyonnaise Potatoes
- Spaghetti Bolognese

Red wine vinegar
- Quorn Vindaloo
- Sweet and Sour Quorn

Rice (long grain)
- Basque Quorn
- Chilli con Quorn with Guacamole
- Hungarian Goulash
- Mole Quorn
- Quorn and Cashew Nuts with Rice
- Quorn Fried Rice
- Quorn Stroganoff
- Stuffed Peppers
- Sweet and Sour Quorn

Rice (Spanish Paella)
- Paella

Rice noodles
- Pad Thai

Rice vinegar
- Singapore Stir Fried Noodles

Rosemary
- Traditional Sunday Roast with Yorkshire Pudding

Saffron
- Italian Casserole with Risotto alla Milanese
- Paella
- Quorn Korma with Pilau Rice and Naan Bread
- Tandoori Quorn with Saffron Rice

Sage
- Traditional Sunday Roast with Yorkshire Pudding

Salt
- American (Hot) Pepperoni Pizza
- Moroccan Spicy Tagine with Flatbread
- Quorn Fajitas
- Quorn Korma with Pilau Rice and Naan Bread
- Quorn Tikka Masala with Rice and Naan Bread
- Quorn Vindaloo

Shiitake mushrooms
- Singapore Stir Fried Noodles

Soured cream
- Chilli con Quorn with Guacamole
- Hungarian Goulash
- Paprika Quorn Fillets
- Quorn Fajitas
- Quorn Stroganoff

Southern Fried Quorn Fillets

Soy sauce
- Quorn and Cashew Nuts with Rice
- Quorn Chow Mein
- Quorn Fried Rice
- Singapore Stir Fried Noodles
- Sweet and Sour Quorn

Spaghetti Bolognese

Spaghetti
- Spaghetti Bolognese

Spring onion
- Quorn Chow Mein
- Quorn Fried Rice
- Singapore Stir Fried Noodles

Stuffed Peppers

Suet (vegetarian)
- Irish Stew and Dumplings
- Quorn in Ale Pudding

Sugar
- American (Hot) Pepperoni Pizza
- Green Curry with Sticky Rice

Sunflower oil
- All recipes!

Swede
- Cornish Pasty

Sweet and Sour Quorn

Tabasco sauce
- Chilli con Quorn with Guacamole
- Quorn Fajitas

Tagliatelle Carbonara

Tagliatelle
- Paprika Quorn Fillets
- Tagliatelle Carbonara

Tamarind paste
- Red Curry with Jasmine Rice

Tandoori Quorn with Saffron Rice

Tartiflette
Thai fish sauce
- Green Curry with Sticky Rice
- Pad Thai
- Red Curry with Jasmine Rice

Thai Jasmine rice
- Red Curry with Jasmine Rice

Thai sticky rice
- Green Curry with Sticky Rice

Thyme
- Bangers and Mash with red wine gravy
- Carbonnade à la Flamande avec Frites
- Lancashire Hotpot
- Quorn in Ale Pudding
- Quorn Bourguignonne with Dauphinois Potatoes
- Quorn au Pot with Boulangère Potatoes
- Quorn au Vin with Lyonnaise Potatoes
- Southern Fried Quorn Fillets
- Traditional Sunday Roast with Yorkshire Pudding

Toad in the Hole
Tomato
- Basque Quorn
- Chilli con Quorn with Guacamole
- Italian Casserole with Risotto alla Milanese
- Quorn Fajitas
- Quorn Madras with Bombay Potatoes
- Quorn Tikka Masala with Rice and Naan Bread

Tomato purée double concentrate
- American (Hot) Pepperoni Pizza
- Basque Quorn
- Chilli con Quorn with Guacamole
- Cottage Pie
- Italian Casserole with Risotto alla Milanese
- Lasagna al Forno
- Moussaka
- Quorn Madras with Bombay Potatoes
- Quorn Tikka Masala with Rice and Naan Bread
- Spaghetti Bolognese

Traditional Sunday Roast with Yorkshire Pudding
Turmeric
- Quorn Biryani
- Quorn Korma with Pilau Rice and Naan Bread
- Quorn Madras with Bombay Potatoes

- Quorn Tikka Masala with Rice and Naan Bread
- Quorn Vindaloo
- Singapore Stir Fried Noodles

Turnip
- Haggis wi' 'tatties an' 'neeps
- Irish Stew and Dumplings
- Quorn au Pot with Boulangère Potatoes

Vermicelli rice noodles
- Singapore Stir Fried Noodles

Vietnamese Noodle Soup

Whisky
- Haggis wi' 'tatties an' 'neeps

Dry white wine
- Italian Casserole with Risotto alla Milanese
- Quorn au Pot with Boulangère Potatoes
- Quorn Risotto
- Quorn Stroganoff
- Tartiflette

Worcestershire Sauce
- Lancashire Hotpot

Yeast (dried)
- American (Hot) Pepperoni Pizza
- Quorn Korma with Pilau Rice and Naan Bread
- Quorn Tikka Masala with Rice and Naan Bread

Yellow Pepper
- Paella

Yoghurt
- Quorn Biryani
- Quorn Korma with Pilau Rice and Naan Bread
- Quorn Tikka Masala with Rice and Naan Bread
- Quorn Vindaloo
- Tandoori Quorn with Saffron Rice

Appendix: Comparing Quorn with Beef, Chicken and Pork

This table shows the comparison values for 100g of Quorn Steak Strips with the same amount of lean beef steak, chicken breast and pork chop.

The percentage figures are the percentage of the guideline daily amounts for a healthy adult of average weight.

	Quorn	**Beef**	**Chicken**	**Pork**
Energy	420 kcal (21%)	194 kcal	110 kcal	250 kcal (13%)
Protein	14.3g	26.9g	22.0g	27.9g
Carbohydrate	4.3g	Negligible	Negligible	Negligible
- of which sugars	1.1g	Negligible	Negligible	Negligible
Fat	1.5g (2%)	8.8g (14%)	2.0g (3%)	14.6g (22%)
- of which saturated fat	1.0g (5%)	3.3g (16%)	1.0g (5%)	5.4g (271%)
Fibre	6.0g	Negligible	Negligible	Negligible

ABOUT THE AUTHOR

Mark Green is a freelance writer, author of the *Impressions* series of travel books, and musician. He has lived in the UK and Holland and has also worked for three years in Paris and Luxembourg. He speaks French, German, Dutch, Spanish and Italian with varying degrees of fluency, depending on how recently he has been in each country. He has travelled widely, visiting at least 60 countries at the last count. He loves good food and wine and likes to try the local cuisine wherever he goes, but he does draw the line at deep fried grasshoppers.

Cover photograph and all other photographs by the author.

Printed in Great Britain
by Amazon